bamboo

DEDICATION

'I hear and I forget.

I see and I remember.

I do and I understand.'

Confucius (551–479 BC)

bamboo

A JOURNEY WITH CHINESE FOOD

SALLY HAMMOND

GORDON HAMMOND

NEW
HOLLAND

THE CHINESE PUZZLE

Just when I think I am beginning to understand China, something happens to make me realise that I have only just begun. It's hard to see and interpret such a rich and complex country in one trip. For centuries a constant stream of inquisitive visitors have returned home with even more questions about China than they set out with.

China is changing at an enormous rate. On each visit we have noticed more relaxed attitudes; for example on the visible control exercised by the police and military. Business people and entrepreneurs are able to exercise their economic and business muscles.

Capitalism sits well with China, there are cautious predictions it will become the world's next super-power, that Shanghai will be the new Wall Street in a couple of decades.

Those of China's 'single-child' generation—indulged (some say spoiled), scrutinised and doted on—are now grown up and producing another generation of children; sometimes with two in the family if they have married another 'single-child'.

Tourists are flooding into China, bringing expectations and the opportunity for locals to try out their language skills. English has become a popular language for young Chinese to learn, and few visitors will leave the country without participating in at least one impromptu language session with an eager local keen to test his or her skills.

Chinese people are travelling too, both within their own country and internationally, absorbing different cultures and in turn being instrumental in changing their own.

Sally Hammond

contents

WELCOME TO CHINA

CHINESE COOKS ARE LIKE FOOD LOVERS ALL OVER THE WORLD—THEY LOVE TO SHARE!

FRIENDS AND EXPERTS IN ALL THE CUISINES OF CHINA HAVE BEEN HAPPY TO SHOW ME THEIR FAVOURITE RECIPES FOR THIS BOOK.

introduction

I always felt there was a mystery about China and I often wondered if I would ever see this ancient country for myself. Yet when I finally had the opportunity to go there I was apprehensive. Would the people be friendly? Was it safe to travel? Most importantly, would I like the food?

Yes, the food! Friends who had already been there shook their heads. 'It's not like the Chinese food we get here,' they told me.

They were right, of course. It wasn't the same, it was so much better! How can anything compare to sitting around a table with a bunch of new-found friends, bending into the steam of a hot pot, dipping paper-thin slices of meat into a rich bubbling broth so that they cook in seconds? Or how about watching a chef shake a lump of dough into a skein of silken noodles in mere minutes?

China has several main cuisine regions and each is different. We have travelled there many times and each time we have become more adventurous. We have shopped in the local markets, asking for advice and for ways to use unfamiliar produce, often taking pictures to remind us how something looked, even how it was made.

I have been tutored in dumpling making by an expert—a Chinese housewife in her own kitchen—and scribbled down my take on other dishes as we were eating, everywhere from trains to top restaurants.

The recipes in this book may call for a trip to a Chinese market or Chinatown to collect some unusual ingredients, but it will be worth it.

My hope is that this book and the dishes in it will inspire you to do even more—to go to this fascinating country and see and taste for yourself!

the menu

APPETISERS

Chicken-filled shiitake mushrooms	118
Deep fried pork pie	129
Steamed Tibetan momos	159
Chinese dumplings	20
with black bean sauce	

MAIN DISHES
MEAT

Hakka meatroll	105
Hakka Yongtaufu	108
Mongolian hot pot	45
Yangzhou lion's head meatballs	67

CHICKEN AND DUCK

Beggar's chicken	74
Spicy chicken with peanuts	148
Peking duck	31
Sichuan chicken and hot peppers	137
Thukpa	172

SEAFOOD

Crispy skin fish	
with sweet and sour sauce	79
Drunken prawns	64
Fish chow mein	54
Fish in wine lees and garlic	34
Hangzhou Lake prawns	
with Longjing tea	70
Lobster in ginger sauce	100

MAIN DISHES
VEGETABLE

Chilli tomato eggs	145
Fish fragrant eggplant	140
Garlic stalks and beef on a train	27
Toffee potatoes	168
Wilted lettuce and cucumber stirfry	113

BREADS

Shanghai onion cakes	61

SOUPS

Codfish soup Macanese style	126
Congee or fish porridge	57
'Crossing the Bridge' noodles	95
Fish dumpling soup	89
Prawn and rice vermicelli soup	130
Tomato and egg soup	41
Winter melon chowder	84

DESSERTS AND SWEET THINGS

Chocolate ginger lychees	96
Mango pudding	125
Portuguese tarts	121
Sweet bird's nest in almond milk	90

OTHER

Tibetan butter tea	162
Rice, boiled and fried	11

THE REGIONS OF CHINA

Northern Region
Eastern Region
Southern Region
Western Region
Far West Region

Kashgar

Jiayuguan

Datong   Beijing

Pingyao

Xiahe   Xian   Shaolin
      Tianshui

Mt Huangshan   Suzhou   Shanghai

Shigatse   Lhasa

Chengdu   Hangzhou

Dequen

Lijiang

Dali   Guilin

Kunming

Guangzhou

Hong Kong
Macau

five facts about China

1   IT IS VAST: China covers an area of 9.5 million square kilometres (3.7 million square miles), with 14,500 kilometres (9,000 miles) of coastline. Elevation varies from 154 metres (505 feet) below sea level at Turpan through to 8.85 kilometres (5.5 miles) above (Mt Everest).

2   SAME TIME ZONE: Despite these distances (and four hour's time difference) from the eastern coast to the western border, officially all of China goes by Beijing time.

3   COMMUNICATION BY PHONE: China's 1.3 billion population uses 263 million fixed phones and a further 269 million mobiles.

4   LANGUAGE: The world's most commonly spoken language is Mandarin with 915 million speakers. There are around 12 languages but there may be up to a thousand dialects. Mandarin has 56,000 characters although only a few thousand are generally used. Pinyin, a way of writing Chinese words using the Roman alphabet, was adopted in 1958.

5   INNOVATION: The Chinese invented the first planetarium, gunpowder, the compass, silk making, printing, paper production, the use of tea, herbal medicine and much more.

WOKS, STEAMBOATS AND CLEAVERS—
THE WORLD OF CHINESE COOKERY

Chinese food has long held a certain mystique for Westerners. And while there are some things we still cannot quite handle—how are you, for instance with chicken's feet, frogs, or fresh snake's blood?—hundreds of other dishes have us well and truly hooked.

Who hasn't fallen for yum cha, that noisy, exuberant, untidy meal that can extend from breakfast through until mid-afternoon? What's not to like about that constant procession of trundling trolleys and trays bearing everything from plates of exquisite dainties, to hefty servings of soup and noodles and rice?

Off the beaten track, in 'outback' China, things may get a little more, well, unsophisticated. Be prepared for street food which might include scorpions and slender snakes threaded onto bamboo sticks, or hunks of cake carved from a huge slab (where are the ovens big enough to bake these monsters?) and iced on the spot for you to take back to your hotel.

In most towns and cities there'll be freshly baked breads, and little filled pies, often cooked at almost cremation heat on the insides of round tandoor-style ovens on the footpath, the magical aromas making them easy to find. Just don't pass on that blood-red drink you'll find in bottles on the footpath sometimes. It's possibly freshly squeezed pomegranate juice, and it is as delicious as it is healthy.

rice

How to Cook Rice

Rice almost triples in quantity when cooked. A cup of dry rice can swell to almost three cups when cooked and serves four or more people. Try using stock or coconut milk for variety when cooking rice.

Cook white rice in plenty of boiling water (salted if liked) for 15 minutes, or until tender, then drain. There should be no need to rinse it. Commercial electric rice-cookers are extremely popular with people who eat rice daily, or a simple plastic one which cooks rice in the microwave, also works well.

Prepare sticky rice by soaking overnight in water to cover, then draining and steaming for 30–45 minutes. The resulting sticky mass is suitable for chilling or cutting into shapes, and for use in recipes that call for it specifically.

FRIED RICE

This is perhaps one of the most basic of all Asian meals and a wonderful way to use up leftovers attractively. For firm separate grains, cook rice the day before and refrigerate it, covered, in a shallow dish overnight or for several hours

To cook, simply heat a little oil in a large pan, add chopped onion, garlic, fresh ginger, chopped chilli, capsicum, mushrooms, and any other vegetables you like. Stir in a beaten egg if desired, mixing it through well, then add cooked or raw chopped meat, chicken or fish, and basically anything else you like.

Stir until everything is heated through, and the meat is cooked and browning. Season to taste with salt or soy sauce and chilli. Again, cook according to your own taste and imagination. Finally add rice and stir to combine it with the other ingredients. Let it heat right though. Watch the bottom of the pan until it sticks—it's fine to keep it a little crispy on the bottom.

Rice Storage

RICE IS EASY TO STORE AND MAY BE KEPT FOR SEVERAL MONTHS IN AN AIRTIGHT CONTAINER IN A COOL, DRY PLACE.

In warmer months it may be refrigerated or stored in the freezer to discourage insect pests. Some varieties from Asian countries may need to be washed before use or checked for stones. Australian rice needs no rinsing.

Once rice has been cooked it should be kept refrigerated and covered. It will keep this way for several days, or it may be frozen successfully for up to a month. The texture may change and become more crumbly so decide whether this will matter in the finished dish or if it is just as easy to cook fresh rice.

Over the centuries, several distinct cuisines have sprung up largely influenced of course by what will grow in each area, as well as the ethnic mix. So in Macau, for example, there is a strong Portuguese influence. In other regions, minority Chinese groups may have put their own cultural stamp on the food, and in other places influences from adjoining countries such as Kazakhstan in the west, or Vietnam and Myanmar in the south show up in various dishes.

Religion plays a part too. Muslim food in the north and west dictates more mutton will be used to take the place of the ubiquitous pork dishes found throughout much of the rest of China.

In places where Buddhists have long been established, vegetarianism or a form of it is popular.

The one thing all Chinese people have in

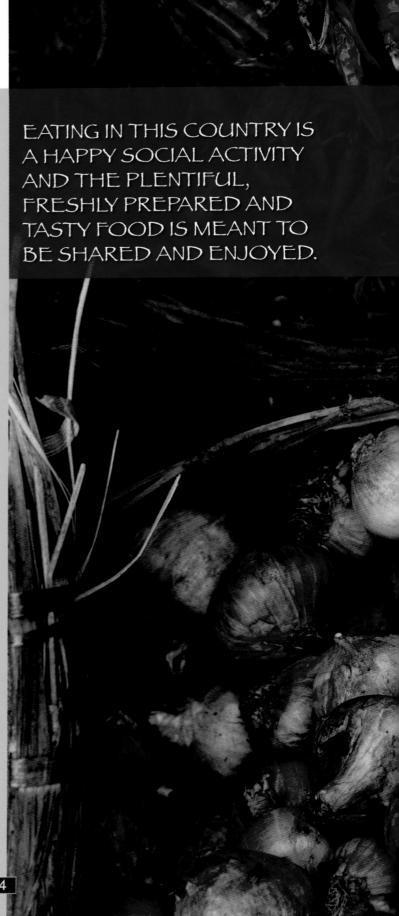

EATING IN THIS COUNTRY IS A HAPPY SOCIAL ACTIVITY AND THE PLENTIFUL, FRESHLY PREPARED AND TASTY FOOD IS MEANT TO BE SHARED AND ENJOYED.

common is that they really like to eat! Eating in this country is a happy social activity and the plentiful, freshly prepared and tasty food is meant to be shared and enjoyed. At any moment of the day you will pass people selecting watermelons or chickens from a market, squatting on the footpath enjoying a bowl of noodles or snacking on packets of seeds or nuts or those other indefinable treats that fill any town's multitude of grocery stores and stalls.

The rest will be seated in groups around steaming hotpots, dipping pieces of meat or vegetables into the bubbling broth, or watching critically as a vendor flips and tosses their order of stir-fried rice or noodles in a wok.

Business deals may be done over banquets in secluded restaurants lushly decorated with red and gold drapes and polished wood panelling, while families gather in large restaurants where the laminex tables and plastic chairs may give little hint of the excellent fare awaiting them.

Tourist groups inevitably find themselves seated at round tables for ten with a large turntable in the middle on which dish after shared dish is set.

It hardly matters how or where you eat in China. Your fellow diners may often prove to be noisy companions, eating rapidly, slurping their noodles enthusiastically, and throwing scraps and bones on the table. It's all part of the routine.

the northern region

FOOD OF THE EMPEROR

BEIJING: CAPITAL CUISINE

BEIJING WAS THE CITY CHOSEN BY CHINA'S RULING CLASSES AS THEIR CAPITAL AND SO YOU WILL FIND A MORE EXTRAVAGANT, MEAT-BASED CUISINE HERE.

Northern or Beijing (Peking) cuisine includes the provinces of Hunan, Shantung, Hopei, Honon, Shansi, Shensi and Inner Mongolia as well as Beijing, formerly known as Peking, and now the capital of the People's Republic of China.

The repertoire evolved with a preference for hearty, no-nonsense dishes, without the heavy spicing or rich sauces found further south. Unfazed by religious limitations they were free to eat anything, although the Mongolian rulers favoured mutton, and many of these traditions persist today.

Onions grow well in the colder north and these are found in many dishes, often stir-fried at the beginning

of a dish. Most hardier crops such as corn, sorghum, wheat, cabbages and root vegetables are grown here and dishes predictably lean towards flour-based dishes such as steamed dumplings and noodles rather than rice.

In the kitchens of the Forbidden City in Beijing, thousands of cooks from the different parts of China once combined their cooking skills in an effort to impress the royal families and officials. This experimentation flowed on to add interest and variety to local menus and finally brought about what is referred to as 'capital city cuisine'.

As the modern capital of China today, Beijing has all the dining options you would find in any major city around the world. Fried snacks from roadside stalls and small shops have long been popular with Beijing's diners.

While many Chinese regard Beijing cuisine as the homeliest, some say the poorest, of China's four major cuisines, two dishes stand out as worth enjoying while in the region.

Crisp-edged slices of Peking duck breast, with a dab of Hoisin sauce and wrapped in paper-thin pancakes is one of life's greater pleasures. Better yet, make your way to a restaurant where there are several courses, each using that same duck in various ways, and you will be a northern cuisine fan forever.

Mongolian hotpot is another not-to-be-missed experience in the north. Plan to take your time, experiment with the various meats and vegetables, noodles and eggs, and finish the meal with a bowl of the stock in which these morsels have been cooked. By then it will be a rich and flavoursome broth, and you will understand why the emperors liked this cuisine so much.

CHINESE DUMPLINGS

There are several traditional fillings for these dumplings. Chopped prawns or turkey mince may be substituted for pork. Serve with condiments such as soy sauce, rice vinegar, black vinegar, chilli sauce, sesame oil, chopped spring onions and mix as desired to create a dipping sauce. While most Chinese home cooks make their own dough and cut it into circles for the dumpling wrappers, using packages of commercial wrappers saves a lot of time and trouble. There are small semi-circular plastic dumpling presses available which make the process of sealing and pleating the dough easier, too.

PORK DUMPLINGS

250g (8oz) ground pork
2 cups chopped Chinese cabbage
1 cup chopped onion or spring onions (scallions)
2 teaspoons finely chopped garlic
½ teaspoon grated ginger
1 tablespoon soy sauce
½ tablespoon sesame oil
½ teaspoon salt
1 egg
1 package dumpling (gow gee) wrappers,
or 40 home-made wrappers

   Combine all the ingredients up to and including the egg in a large bowl and stir well. Drop a teaspoonful of filling into the centre of a wrapper, fold in half to make a semicircle, then gently pleat edges to seal and make an attractive edge. Continue until all the filling has been used. Heat one tablespoon of oil in a frying pan on medium heat. In batches, arrange the dumplings in the pan and cook until browning on the base. Add enough water or stock to cover the base of the pan. Cook on medium-low heat for five minutes or until the liquid evaporates.
   Serve with Black Bean Sauce (see page 22)

MAKES 40 DUMPLINGS (ENOUGH FOR 3-4 PEOPLE)

Note: Instead of frying, dumplings may be dropped into a large pan of boiling water and simmered until done (they will float) about 3-5 minutes.

on the north-eastern edge of the Tibetan plateau, and many kilometres from Lhasa, we visited one of the largest lamaseries (monasteries) in China. It is home to hundreds of monks and luckily we arrived just in time for a special ceremony. Enthralled we watch as the maroon-clad monks wearing high curving headgear, removed their cosy knee-length black felt boots and filed inside the temple. There, seated on low cushions, they chanted to the clashing music as they sipped yak butter tea.

Yet this was tame compared to another festival we witnessed far west at a monastery in Shigatse, in Tibet proper. The music began almost as soon as we were seated and the programme filled the morning with colour and movement. Monks wearing red and gold and purple scarves paraded past. Some swung censers, others wore impressive gaudy papier mâché animal heads. There were troupes of masked performers, even clowns, winding up with the star turn of the day: several monks playing enormous brass horns in a mournful, deafening two-note fanfare.

China's multicultural multi-layered society

means that any turn can bring you face to face with action. A martial arts demonstration, opera singers with white painted faces on stage beside a busy intersection, boys throwing down strings of red crackers in the street or a full-blown display to celebrate something or other.

In one city we woke at midnight to fireworks erupting for no apparent reason far across town.

That's OK. China doesn't need an excuse for celebrations.

PEKING DUCK

The process for making Peking Duck is lengthy and involves scalding the skin of a whole bird with head still attached, then basting, drying and roasting before the dish everyone loves can be served. Even in China, it is rarely prepared at home. Diners usually go to special restaurants where the rest of the bird features in a series of other dishes on the menu. The process originated in Beijing (then Peking) during the Yuan dynasty (1206–1368) and became a favourite of the imperial family in the Ming dynasty. Barbecued duck is available from most Chinese BBQ shops and restaurants.

peking duck wrappers*
Chinese barbecued duck, fat separated and sliced,
meat cut in thin slices
soy sauce, Hoisin sauce and chilli sauce for dipping
thin strips of cucumber and spring onions (shallot/scallions)

Warm the wrappers, covered, on a very low heat in the oven or microwave. Keep warm and covered. Each diner then takes a slice of duck skin and fat and dips it into their choice of sauces. It is then placed on a wrapper along with a slice of cucumber and spring onion. The bottom edge of the wrapper is folded up and then rolled before eating. Once the skin has been used, then the meat is eaten in the same way.

*Available from Chinese and Asian supermarkets.

MARKET FORCES

I am not generally squemish, but some of the offerings in the Wangfujiang Street night market in Beijing made me shudder.

Seeing my reticence, the attendant behind the table grinned and picked up a centipede as if to throw it at me.

It wasn't that bad, I suppose. He could have lobbed a scorpion, some silkworms or a snake at me. They were there for sale too, although most of them were securely threaded onto skewers ready for their appointment with the grill as soon as someone was brave enough to order them. It was quite obvious we were in the minority as everyone else was drooling at the offerings.

Trade was brisk and the others, Chinese all of them, were eagerly ordering the grisly kebabs, or some other dainty—heaps of noodles, chunks of tofu, dim sum—and something I did like the look of, slices of fruit embedded in toffee, glowing like stained glass.

Our guide had told us a joke just that day and now we really got it. 'Were Adam and Eve Chinese?' he'd asked, then answered it himself. 'No, because if they had been, they would have eaten the snake first, and then the apple.'

Markets are the core of Chinese cookery. Every region, every province, every town has its weekly, often daily market. They are constant surprises. You turn a corner and there on the roadside, often spilling over onto part of the road, are barrows and stalls and baskets of produce, including fish.

In one place it was spring onions (shallots/scallions), the biggest I have ever seen, a metre or more in length, loaded onto the backs of tractors and trucks. In a dusty part of Szechuan we followed horsemen selling bushels of red chillies to a market; elsewhere it was strings of garlic slung from every wall. At Urumqi we browsed an endless selection

铁板鱿鱼
香酥鸡排

of trays of sultanas, dried fruit and roasted salted nuts still in the shell. In the Muslim west we passed a meat market with vats of boiled sheep's heads, whole carcasses hanging ready for dismemberment, and bowls and trays of gleaming innards. In remote Kashgar we could have bought a camel or a donkey.

Almost always close at hand to these markets is fresh and tempting street food so you can shop for dinner and pick up a pastry or a dumpling for lunch at the same time.

Duck eggs, watermelons, oranges or offal, anything is available. Anyone for a grilled centipede?

FISH IN WINE LEES
AND GARLIC

500g (1lb) thick white fish fillets
1 egg white, lightly beaten
3 teaspoons cornflour
1 piece dried wood ear mushroom, soaked for 30 minutes
   in hot water
1½ cups (375ml/12fl oz) vegetable or peanut oil
2 teaspoons wine lees (or 1 tablespoon rice wine)
1 teaspoon salt
1½ tablespoons sugar
2 garlic cloves, peeled and thinly sliced
1 cup (250ml/8fl oz) chicken stock
1 tablespoon cornflour, extra

Cut the fish into about 8 pieces. Place in dish and add the egg white
and 3 teaspoons cornflour and stir around until coated.

Drain the wood ear mushroom and roll up. Cut into fine shreds, then
chop into tiny pieces.

Heat the oil in a wok and when very hot carefully slide in the fish to
cook for about 20 seconds.

Remove with a slotted spoon and set aside.

Drain off the oil and return 1 tablespoon to the wok. Combine the
wine lees or rice wine, salt and sugar in a small bowl.

Reheat and fry the garlic until lightly golden. Add the wine lees
mixture, the stock and the chopped mushroom, and add the fish.
Simmer gently.

Stir the extra cornflour into 1½ tablespoons cold water and stir into
the sauce to thicken.

Serve immediately.

SERVES 4

Recipe © Jacki Passmore, used with permission.

OODLES OF NOODLES

MARCO POLO GETS THE CREDIT FOR INTRODUCING PASTA TO ITALY. IT'S A NICE STORY, BUT NO ONE WILL EVER KNOW IF IT IS TRUE OR NOT. SOME SAY POLO'S STORY WAS A FANCIFUL WISH-LIST DREAMED UP BY AN ARMCHAIR TRAVELLER. IN SHORT, HE MAY NEVER EVEN HAVE VISITED ALL THE PLACES HE DOCUMENTED.

Who knows? The facts state that by 960AD specialty noodle shops abounded in China, and as early as 1200AD there were rules in Italy governing the size and shape of noodles. Interestingly, long before young Marco is said to have visited China, by 500BC the inventive Etruscans had devised all the standard equipment needed for making it.

While there are about 650 different shapes and sizes of Italian pasta, Asian nations have a wealth of other varieties ranging from spring roll wrappers and wonton skins to fine transparent

IT SEEMS THAT THERE IS HARDLY A GRAIN OR VEGETABLE THAT CAN'T BE TURNED INTO PASTA OR NOODLES.

mung bean threads, straight soba sticks, coils of egg noodles and skeins of rice noodles. It seems that there is hardly a grain or vegetable that can't, with patience, be turned into pasta or noodles.

In the Old City of Shanghai we stopped by a viewing window and watched a team of white coated chefs expertly rolling and filling and pinching dumplings that would be steamed and served immediately to the long line of eager customers waiting by a small serving counter in the wall. It was labour intensive but the rhythm of the workers made it almost ballet-like in its choreography.

In other parts of China I have watched in wonder as a chef performs magic. No matter how many times I see it done—a shapeless chunk of dough transformed in a couple of minutes into a hank of slinky perfect strands of noodles—to me it is

as incomprehensible as any theatre act with smoke and mirrors.

And yet it appears so simple. Hold an end of the piece of dough in each hand. Bring your hands together, flip the dough somehow, twist it, draw your hands apart stretching the dough—now showing two lengths—then repeat and repeat and repeat until like a conjuror, you've turned it into a skein of tender noodles, the makings of a soup or stir-fry.

As I said, pure magic.

BEAN FOOD

TOFU OR BEAN CURD—THE CHINESE CALL IT DOU-FU MEANING 'ROTTEN BEANS'—HAS BEEN ON CHINESE TABLES SINCE 260BC.

It is made from soaked soy beans that are crushed and strained to form a milky liquid. This soy milk is then coagulated using seawater or nigari (magnesium chloride from seawater) or even gypsum, a type of plaster of paris, to produce a sort of non-dairy cottage cheese.

Tofu needs to be used in flavoursome dishes (think stir-fries, soups and curries) otherwise it is boring. However, its firm but not chewy texture also makes it a useful stand-in for chicken or other tender meats in dishes. The Chinese use it extensively, either for meatless dishes or in conjunction with meats.

Soy beans, one of the five ancient grains and originally grown over 2000 years ago in China, were known as 'meat of the earth'. Their use was first recorded by Emperor Shen Nung in 2800BC but Europe was much later in finding out about them. They did not arrive there until 1712. While still comparatively under-utilised by Westerners, soy beans are valued by vegetarians as a source of a valuable vegetable protein with a wide variety of uses. It is a major crop in China and north-eastern Asia and grown extensively in cooler, drier climates.

I am always on the alert for tofu when travelling in China. Often I sight pieces of it bobbing in soups, or its undisguisable whiteness flecking chilli dishes and vegetable stir fries. Sometimes it is fried and often only the square edges of the cubes or slices alert me that these are not simply pieces of fish or chicken.

Once tofu has been soaked in broths or sauces it tends to absorb fiery or subtle flavours alike—making it absolutely delicious..

THE GREAT WALL OF
CHINA WAS NOT BUILT TO
KEEP OUT RABBITS!

THE GREAT WALL

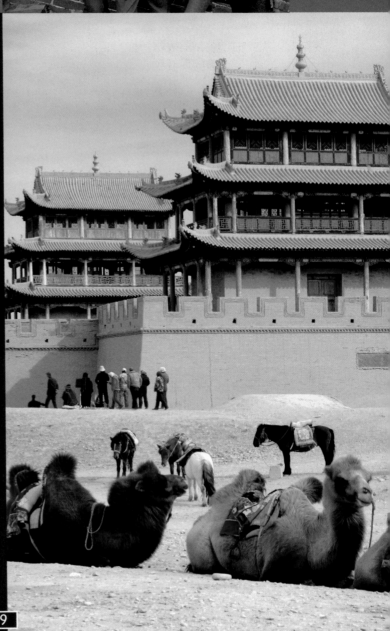

Hiking along the uneven surface of the Great Wall, we were accosted near a watchtower by a group of several Chinese tourists. 'May we take photo?'

Did they want Gordon to take a picture of them, we asked?

'No, no,' they assured us. They wanted a picture of him. With them. A trophy-tourist, it seemed. Their companion with just a little English explained: 'They are from the country. They have never seen a Westerner before.'

Contrary to a popular TV ad, the Great Wall of China was not built to keep out rabbits. In the many centuries BC something far more sinister was lurking to the north—barbarian bandits.

TOMATO AND EGG SOUP

Soups in China appear after the main meal, and are seen as a good way to ensure that diners have had enough to eat. This soup appears in so many parts of the country, no doubt because it is so quick and easy, the ingredients are generally available, and it tastes so good.

2 eggs
pinch of salt
5 cups (1.25l/2pts) hot water
3cm (1in) root ginger, peeled and bruised
2 large tomatoes, peeled and cut in 8 wedges
finely chopped spring onions (shallots/scallions) to garnish

Beat eggs with the pinch of salt until well mixed. Place the water in a large pan with the ginger and another good pinch of salt. Heat until simmering, then pour in the beaten eggs, stirring gently so that they form threads. Add the tomatoes and remove the pan from the heat after a minute. Season to taste, remove the ginger, and garnish with chopped spring onions.

SERVES 4

Barbarian bandits had formed a nasty habit of sneaking in and stealing the local treasures and later the goodies so laboriously transported thousands of kilometres from central Asia and eastern Europe on the Silk Road; or the priceless silk which had been prepared in readiness to head west for sale.

Of course the Great Wall's days of being a defensive outpost have long gone. Today hundreds of thousands of visitors each year marvel at its endless serpentine loops—and, no, these cannot be seen from outer space—yet this structure, which took almost 2000 years to build, and stretches over six thousand kilometres east to west, still amazes all who see it.

More than that it has become a magnet for locals and tourists. Who would dare visit Beijing and not take a day trip to the Wall?

While the stretch closest to the capital is the part most visitors experience, we were to spot sections of it in many places as we travelled.

Occasionally, spotted from a train window, it was just a dusty turret on the horizon; at other times we saw it winding off into the distance and couldn't help but try to imagine what it must have been like to labour on its construction. Generations would have spent their lives and energies sweating it out

AMONGST THE WARRIORS

THE TERRACOTTA WARRIORS WERE FIRED IN THE QIN DYNASTY AND HAD BEEN BURIED FOR OVER 2000 YEARS.

Gordon and I were lucky enough to gain official permission (and a watchful guide) to walk amongst a section of the terracotta warriors at X'ian. Not gazing down on them from above, but actually standing beside them, looking into their vacant eyes, inspecting their scars of battle—well the injuries inflicted by centuries of entombment—and wondering not only at their chance discovery, but also about what inspired such an ambitious project in the first place.

In March 1974, Mr Yang, a pomegranate orchardist, was digging a well on his property near X'ian, the official beginning of the Silk Road. He was perplexed when his spade hit something he had never seen before. No wonder. The Terracotta Warriors, as they became known, were fired in the Qin dynasty, and had been buried for over 2000 years.

It's hard to imagine why an emperor would commission such a task for his tomb. Around 700 craftsmen are said to have been employed to make these figures which are still being dug up and pieced together. These skilled artisans worked in pairs, fashioning the soldiers' features to match each other's faces.

The figures were created larger than life to show their status, then fired in massive charcoal heated kilns.

Six thousand or so warriors have been exhumed and they lie or stand in various stages of repair in a huge auditorium. Who knows how many more there are? The air inside is thick with the dust raised by the archaeologists as they tediously put together the world's biggest and most intricate jigsaw.

Our brush with fame was well monitored by officials—of course. Just weeks before, we were told, a tourist dressed to resemble a warrior had cunningly inserted himself amongst the figures. He was discovered and unceremoniously removed, to the amusement of the watching crowd.

Yet as we slowly moved amongst them, being SO careful not to knock or touch them, we had the eerie feeling that there was life here too. I had the unnerving impression that at any moment one might clear his throat or gently tap me on the shoulder. It was as if their creators had left them with more than just their own appearance.

Seven million people come here each year to gaze in wonder on this clay army, lined up in rigid ranks. What tales would they have to tell if they could speak? For a moment, I almost thought one might.

PINGYAO

PINGYAO IS NOT LARGE BY CHINESE STANDARDS. IT HAS A POPULATION OF 40,000, AND IS 90 KILOMETRES FROM THE PROVINCIAL CAPITAL, TAIYUAN.

Shaped a little like a stolid turtle with 6.4 kilometres of fortifications on all sides (3.9 miles), it has six city gates and two twenty-metre tall (65 feet) towers.

Inside the gates, on foot, we had the street to ourselves again. On one corner we paused to admire a harlequin-dressed photo-opportunity monkey on a man's shoulder.

I walked on slowly, stopping occasionally to poke and prod strange foods, then watched as a group of women with chopsticks picked over a heap of pig-meat on a table in the street, carefully sorting out edible scraps from everything else.

Two little girls playing nearby on a

doorstep were so busy they didn't even notice when we photographed them.

Our guide suggested we walk along some of the wall with him, and from this vantage point, eight to twelve metres up (26-39 feet), Pingyao was simply a sea of grey tile roofs.

For lunch we stopped at a small meticulously clean cafe which served food which had been freshly prepared just for us, a treat after the mass-produced dishes usually served to bus tour groups in immense restaurants. I understood why the meat was so good when we learned that Pingyao is noted for its fine beef.

Pingyao is remarkably well-preserved. The 14th-century buildings begun in the Ming dynasty were painstakingly restored in the 1990s. There are more than 3000 shops, as well as streets and markets frozen in time. It is now regarded as one of the four best-

preserved ancient cities in China, and in 1997 was added to the UNESCO World Cultural Heritage list.

Nearby, we took time to visit the Qiao Family Compound now preserved as a government museum. 'Raising the Red Lantern' was filmed here in 1991, and more recently (in 2006) a popular TV series was set there too. As we walked in the rose gardens we watched groups of people posing for photographs in front of the stars' posters on the walls.

Old and new; traditional and contemporary. China embraces it all effortlessly, and serves it up without fuss or fanfare, simply inviting the world to visit and see for itself.

the eastern region

SHANGHAI CUISINE: SWEET AND SAUCY

SHANGHAI SIZZLE

THE CITIES OF SHANGHAI AND HANGZHOU HOLD POWERFUL POSITIONS FLANKING THE MOUTH OF THE MIGHTY YANGTSE RIVER.

They are at the crossroads, climatically, between north and south, and this region produces and uses both wheat and rice in its cuisine.

It's a culinary bridge, if you like, between the wheat- flour dominated noodle and dumpling dishes of the north and the rice-based ones of the south, with the obvious addition of many varieties of the local seafood which is abundant in the lakes and rivers of the area.

Eastern or Shanghai Cuisine includes the provinces of Kiangsu, Chekiang, Anhwei and Fukien. However one thing characterises all eastern cooking even more, and that is the liberal use of sugar to sweeten dishes and which works to intensify savoury flavours, especially when used in addition to the ubiquitous soy sauce. This is the famous 'red-cooking', the process of slowly simmering meat in dark soy sauce, and the resultant reddish tinge of the dish.

Congee—a rice gruel similar to porridge and eaten for breakfast throughout China—originated in the south-eastern province of Fukien. This is, strictly speaking, Hakka or Hokkien food, a distinct style of cookery which is found extensively in the southern region, as well as Singapore and Taiwan.

Food in the east is generally lighter and less oily than in the north, and wines and vinegar add complex flavours to many dishes while complementing the sweetness. Eastern cuisine is also known for its use of alcohol in cooking, so dishes such as drunken prawns or drunken chicken paired with salted meats and preserved vegetables attract attention when they appear on menus.

Shanghai has a rich history of international trade and emigrants and this is apparent in the appearance of Russian 'zakuski' (cold appetizers) on menus and French and British influences in some other dishes. In this very large city street food is always popular. Locals queue up at popular stalls selling fried or steamed pork-filled buns and dumplings which are dipped into black vinegar before eating. Deep fried bread is another favourite.

In fact Eastern cuisine has many unusual aspects. Beggar's chicken, wrapped in lotus leaves and covered in clay before baking, necessitates a sure hand in cracking the hard coating so diners may instantly inhale the steamy fragrant aromas of the dish and enjoy the succulent flesh, baked, as if in its own personal oven.

Then there are those strangely unappealing-looking 1000-year-old eggs and another local favourite—something called, unappealingly, 'stinky tofu'.

FISH CHOW MEIN

This dish is a real mixture of many delicious flavours. A complete 'meal-in-a-dish'.

250g (9oz) fine egg noodles

2cm (¾in) knob fresh ginger,
    peeled and crushed

1 tablespoon soy sauce

1 tablespoon oil

500g (1lb) firm white fish fillets,
    cut into 2cm (¾in) squares

2 eggs

oil to fry

½ small cauliflower, thinly sliced

1 medium carrot, thinly sliced

6 dried shiitake mushrooms, soaked, drained,
    stems discarded, thinly sliced

reserved soaking liquid from mushrooms

salt to taste

1 tablespoon cornflour

2 teaspoons soy sauce

½ teaspoon sesame oil

¼ teaspoon sugar (optional)

pepper to taste

Cook noodles for one minute in boiling salted water. Drain and set aside. Mix ginger, soy sauce and oil and marinate the fish in this for 15 minutes. Beat eggs and cook in a frypan or wok until set, like an omelette. Remove from pan and cut into strips. Heat more oil in the frypan, add noodles. Do not stir, but allow to form a 'cake'.

Cook for 3 minutes, on each side. Drain. Saute vegetables and mushrooms for 2 minutes, then add 2 tablespoons reserved mushroom liquid and cook for 1 minute. Pour over noodles. Mix together cornflour, soy sauce, ½ cup (125ml/4fl oz) reserved mushroom liquid, sesame oil, sugar if using, and pepper and set aside. Saute fish in a little oil until tender. Add cornflour mixture and cook until thickened. Pour over noodles and garnish with egg strips.

SERVES 4

SLOW BOATS

SHANGHAI, TEN KILOMETRES (SIX MILES) FROM THE MOUTH OF THE YANGTSE, IS CHINA'S SHOWPLACE, PREDICTED BY SOME TO SOON BECOME THE WORLD'S FINANCIAL HUB.

The rock-solid Bund and colonial buildings on one side of the river contrast with the futuristic spiked and bobbled skyline of its Manhattan-like structures opposite, and a slew of glitzy shopping centres and hotels nearby.

Gordon and I decided to take a trip on the water. The Huangpu river bisects the city, separating the new Pudong area from the more staid Bund. Fortunately, our ferry trip had been slotted in at the end of a round of sightseeing.

We'd begun the day with a 45-second express trip in the lift to the viewing area at the top of the 88-floor Jin Mao Tower which dominates Pudong, and indeed the whole of downtown Shanghai. From there we could look down on the world's highest hotel lobby, the Grand Hyatt on the 54th floor.

Next, a ride to the airport on Shanghai's superfast train, the Maglev (magnetic levitation)

which for a few seconds reaches 430 kph. It spends the rest of the seven-minute trip getting up to speed and slowing down again, and is a truly a 'mouth open in amazement' experience, yet remarkably smooth and quiet.

We were beginning to think that Shanghai is obsessed with speed, which might be true as it is certainly fast-tracking to become a world player in all things financial. No, make that a world leader. The next generation of Shanghainese are hot on the heels of their counterparts in any country, and overtaking fast.

We were ready for some quiet respite, and found it at lunch in Old Shanghai, an enclave of lovingly restored Ming dynasty (14th–17th century) buildings, and followed that with a late afternoon ferry ride. As we climbed aboard and settled down on simple plastic seats ready for a leisurely ride upriver, we remembered that not too far from this ferry terminal, a tunnel (the locals call it the 'tourist tunnel') scoots under the river.

We had taken that on another visit, and I still remember the cartoon-like experience, with bright coloured lights and images flashing on the walls as we zoomed along in little carriages. Shanghai may work hard, but it obviously knows how to have fun too.

The rays of the sun caught the many facets of Pudong's buildings, gleaming first on the face of one then, as we moved past, rolling on to turn another one gold or silver or even sunset pink, before frosting the next one with light. First the Shanghai International Convention Centre flanked by twin globes, complementing the magenta-bobbled Orient Pearl TV Tower building behind got the treatment, then the magic silver wire and glass Jin Mao Tower.

In today's glossy city, it is hard to imagine that the word it donated to English—'shanghai'—had such an unsavoury derivation. It referred, of course, to the bar filled with pretty girls which was once used to lure men who were then abducted and put to use as coolie slaves.

CONGEE OR FISH PORRIDGE

Don't be put off by the name of this. You do not have to eat it for breakfast, although if you did, you would be well set up for the day. Think of it rather as a nutritious fish stew for any meal.

½ cup rice
2 tablespoons oil
6 cups (1.5L/2½pts) water
300g (10½oz) firm white fish, thinly sliced
2 teaspoons soy sauce
1 teaspoon sesame oil
½ teaspoon salt (optional)
pepper to taste
1 cup dried rice vermicelli
oil to fry
6cm (2½ in) piece fresh ginger, shredded finely
1 spring onion (shallots/scallions), finely chopped
1 tablespoon finely chopped coriander

Place rice, oil and water in a large saucepan. Allow to boil, then reduce heat and simmer for 1½ hours. Marinate fish in a mixture of soy sauce, sesame oil, salt and pepper. Fry vermicelli in a little hot oil, drain and reserve until needed. Place boiling rice porridge in individual serving bowls. Top with fish slices and ginger. Garnish with spring onions, coriander and pepper and fried vermicelli.

SERVES 4–6

SILKEN SECRETS

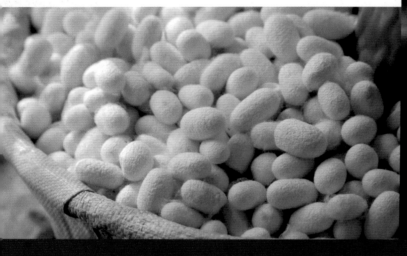

AT THE SILK AND DYEING CENTRE IN SUZHOU, NEAR SHANGHAI, WE FINALLY MET THOSE RESPONSIBLE FOR ASIA'S MOST LUCRATIVE AND ANCIENT INDUSTRY.

In a small display basket a dozen or so ordinary looking grubs crawl around slowly, chomping hungrily on their bed of mulberry leaves. They don't look important at all, yet they are the basis of China's multi-million dollar silk industry, which itself was the result of a bored empress's vivid imagination and the rest of the world's greed for the resulting shimmering fabrics.

Yet the leap between grub and garment is eggs on mulberry leaves, then nurture the silkworms so that they spin soft egg-shaped white cocoons.

These are harvested, then carefully sorted by women working at long conveyor belts in the mill. Double pupae (you can hear them rattling together inside) are put aside for quilt making, the singles go on to be used for spinning. Each pupa has 1.5 kilometres of silk thread on it, yet it takes 4000 to make a 45-centimetre scarf, we were told. If I hadn't written it down at the time I would not believe it.

Hypo-allergenic silk quilts, impossible for tourists to resist (judging by the visitors we saw walking out with identical carry bags) are around 80 layers thick, each gossamer sheet the product of ten cocoons and stretched gently out by a team of

The process doesn't stop here—it's only the beginning. Next the cocoons pass to another worker — and her job I would not like. In a pot of boiling water right beside her they are now cooked. When they are done, she uses a sharp-bristled brush to snare the ends of the silk so the cocoon can be unwound, then deftly attaches the threads onto a spindle that feeds a number of spinning spools above her head.

It's a women-only mill, we were told, as female fingers are better suited to the task. It is steamy, finicky work. The silken thread is then passed to looms where the intricate process of dyeing and weaving begins, transforming it into those delicate and lustrous fabrics which the world loves.

In ancient times, when the Silk Road was at its height, western rulers lusted after silk to create costumes for their courts—and for the battlefield. Some thought the sun flashing on silken pennants would terrify their opponents.

They also thought then that silk grew on trees, so those savvy Chinese kept their valuable secret for centuries.

And what about the cooked pupa at the centre of each cocoon? Nothing is wasted in China. We found them for sale later in the food markets!

SHANGHAI ONION CAKES

1½ cups (190g/6oz) plain flour
sesame oil
salt flakes
4 large green onions, green parts only, chopped
½ cup (125ml/4fl oz) vegetable oil

Sift the flour into a bowl and make a well in the centre. Bring a kettle of water to the boil and pour 3/4 cup (185ml/6fl oz) into the flour. Quickly work into the flour using the handle of a wooden spoon. Work to a smooth, soft dough, then invert the bowl and leave to cool.

When cool enough to handle, knead for 2-3 minutes until smooth. Form into a smooth ball, rub with sesame oil and cover. Leave for 1 hour. Cut the dough into 3-5 pieces and roll out thinly on a lightly floured board.

Brush with sesame oil, sprinkle with salt flakes and evenly cover with chopped onion greens. Roll up, then coil each roll into a round cake. Dust with flour and gently flatten with a rolling pin to about 1cm (1/3in) thick. Heat a flat pan and add the oil. Fry the onion cakes on medium heat until golden brown, turning once or twice.

Recipe © Jacki Passmore, used with permission.

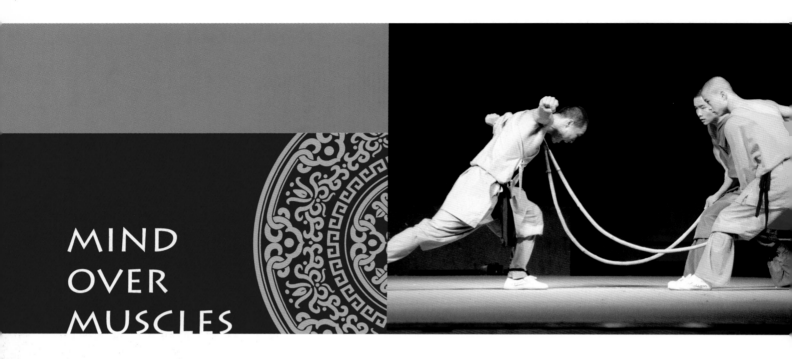

MIND
OVER
MUSCLES

I FLINCHED AS A YOUNG MAN USING ONLY HIS MIND AND MUSCLES FORCED TWO LONG POLES INTO A U-SHAPE. NOT HARD? PERHAPS NOT, EXCEPT HE HAD PLANTED THE ENDS IN HIS NECK, JUST ABOVE HIS COLLARBONE.

We were at Shaolin, birthplace of Chinese martial arts, and this was the tourist show delivered at the Gung Fu Institute by the Shaolin monks. Their creed expresses it like this:

It's not about fighting, it's about balance.
It's not about enlightenment, it's about balance.
It's not about balance ...

So what was it about? We watched, incredulous as groups of young men performed incredible acts of speed, strength and daring. Lots of aggressive

shouting and impossible feats. You could cut the testosterone in the auditorium with a knife—preferably a curved, flat-bladed one, it seemed.

Elsewhere in China, we had seen even more violent displays of martial arts. Metal bars snapped on participants' bald heads, bunches of rods smashed through by a well placed hand chop. They were real too, not papier mâché props. We fingered the remains of them, just to be sure, in a basket in the foyer as we left the hall.

Later, as we walked back to our bus that day we met troops of flag-carrying students dressed in red and black, marching off to one of the many practice fields.

This 'small town', (population 100,000) has 83 Kung Fu schools (the biggest one has 10,000 students) 30,000 students overall, and we seemed to pass most of them. They were all young, scarcely more than children, and included a few girls.

Yet despite the collective strength and potential of the hundreds of uniformed youth around us, I must admit I have never felt safer. They were truly well-trained and fearless company.

Nearby, Mount Songshan, one of China's most sacred mountains casts a benign shadow over the fifth-century Zen Buddhist Shaolin Temple where some gingko trees in the shady compound are reputed to be over 1500 years old. Martial arts students can stay at the temple for a nominal fee and help with cleaning in return and I watched as a shaven-headed teenage monk practised high kicks and leaps against an ancient obelisk.

In a stall at the gate, targeting tourists like us, I could have bought tiny bald figurines, far too chubby for real martial artists, in various intimidating poses, clutching sticks and swords and chains.

Out of place? As the masters say, 'It's about balance. It's not about balance...'

DRUNKEN PRAWNS

Pauline Loh explains: This recipe uses fresh prawns (shrimps). The herbs we use are mild enough, except the strong-tasting 'danggui', or Chinese angelica root. 'Beiqi' and the red boxthorn berries are common tonic herbs. The wine makes this dish a little spicy, but gives the broth a delicious fragrance.

Any Chinese yellow wine will do, but I chose the lovely aged Shaoxing wine called 'nu'er hong', or 'virgin red'.

The story goes that in certain Chinese villages where they produce Shaoxing, parents of a newborn daughter will set a few jars of new wine aside. This is aged until the daughter is ready to be married, and on her wedding day, the casks are broken and served at the marriage feast.

And because their daughter supposedly goes to the marriage bed a virgin, the wine is named after the blushing bride. It's a pretty appropriate name for our dish as well, since the prawns, too, blush bright red as they cook.

PRAWNS IN 'VIRGIN RED' WINE

Use tiger prawns for this dish. They have a better colour and firmer texture which will go well with the strong flavours of the herbal broth. The little bright red boxthorn seeds are also known as wolfberries and are widely available at Asian grocery stores or supermarkets.

3 small slices danggui
6–8 slices beiqi (Chinese herb)
2 cups (500ml/16fl oz) water
a handful of boxthorn berries (about 20)
500g (1lb) large tiger prawns (shrimps)
1 cup (250ml/8fl oz) nu'er hong
    or any Shoaxing wine

Wash and rinse herbs, pat dry. Add water, the herbs and the berries to a pot. Bring to a boil and simmer for 10 minutes.

Trim off feelers and legs from prawns. Remove one segment of shell, the one nearest the head. Keep the rest of the shell on. Set aside.

Add wine to the simmering herbal broth. Add the prawns. Do not allow to boil. Simmer prawns in herbal broth for about 8–10 minutes depending on their size.

They are ready when the heads are thoroughly pink. Transfer to a claypot and serve with a soy sauce and chilli dip.

Recipe © Pauline Loh, used with permission. www.cuisine-asia.com

YANGZHOU LION'S HEAD MEATBALLS

700g (1½lb) slightly fatty pork

2cm (¾in) piece fresh ginger,
  peeled and coarsely chopped

3 garlic cloves, peeled

4 green onions, trimmed and coarsely chopped

1 small can water chestnuts, drained

½ cup cornflour

½ cup (125ml/4fl oz) light soy sauce

1 cup (250ml/8fl oz) vegetable oil

500g (1lb) Chinese white cabbage (wombok)

2 cups (500ml/16fl oz) chicken or pork stock

¼ cup (60ml/2fl oz) rice wine

salt and white pepper, to taste

Cut the pork into cubes, then grind to a reasonably smooth paste in a food processor. Remove and set aside.

In the food processor chop the ginger, garlic, onions and water chestnuts until coarsely chopped.

Return the pork and add 1 tablespoon of the cornflour and half the soy sauce. Process until smooth and sticky. With wet hands, form into four large meatballs.

In a shallow bowl combine the remaining cornflour and soy sauce, adding 1-2 teaspoons of water to make a smooth liquid.

Heat a wok over high heat. Add the vegetable oil and heat. Working one at a time coat the meatballs in the cornflour mixture and slip into the hot oil. Fry, turning as needed and handling them carefully, until the surface is lightly browned, 2½ to 3 minutes.

Using a wire skimmer or slotted spoon, transfer the balls to a Chinese sand-pot or casserole suitable for the stove top.

Reserve the remaining soy-cornflour mixture.

Cut the white parts of the cabbage into 1cm (½in) wide slices and leaves into 4cm (1½in) wide slices.

Reduce the heat of the wok.

Add the cabbage to the hot oil and fry briefly until just wilted. With tongs spread around the pork balls in the casserole.

Add the wine and hot stock, salt and pepper and place over medium heat. Cover tightly and simmer for about 45 minutes, until the 'lion's heads' are tender. Stir up the reserved cornflour and soy sauce mixture and add to the sauce to thicken. Simmer gently for 1–2 minutes. Serve in the pot.

SERVES 4–8

Recipe © Jacki Passmore, used with permission.

TEA FIT FOR AN EMPEROR

A green and yellow banner hanging from a corner of the Hu Xin Ting tea house in Shanghai's Old City catches our eye. 'TEA' it announces. The tourists flock here, but mostly only for a moment to snap a picture before heading off for the shops. It's the locals who come and sit for hours, sipping cup after cup of green, jasmine or flower tea, and soaking up the filtered sunshine which splashes through ornate carved window frames fashioned over 400 years ago.

There are many teahouses in this elegantly restored area and so we took the lift to one that overlooks the zigzag bridge across the lake. Here we sipped green tea and absorbed the busyness below from our quiet vantage point.

It takes much practice to master the various hand positions and steps necessary to elegantly carry out the complicated and formal presentation of the ancient and complex ritual of a tea ceremony.

Even though the Gongfu (Chinese) tea ceremony is more relaxed than the Japanese one, there are still many important steps. At one teahouse our hostess expertly rinsed each teapot, 'nourishing it' she said, and tutored us carefully through tastings of several teas: green, oolong (once only drunk by emperors) and jasmine. It was as if time stood still in that cool and shuttered place. We had entered another, less stressful era.

In every Chinese city, teahouses—like cafés in Europe—are central to life. In China though, most people come for the ambience rather than a quick caffeine hit. Here, amongst polished wood and bamboo screens, they can relax with their friends or chat over mah-jong or cards.

It is said that in the seventh century the Chinese added salt to their tea which they felt balanced the diuretic effect of the drink. Today, it is drunk as it comes. No milk. No sugar. The etiquette of tea houses is just as basic.

Apart from the tea ceremony, a visit is reassuringly low-key. Seated on low stools or wooden chairs, patrons may stay as long as they wish, refill their cups almost endlessly and—a noisy slurp is actually expected. It is said to aerate the tea and intensify the flavour.

It is traditional for cups to be only 70 per cent filled because the Chinese say this amount represents friendship. The remaining unseen 30 per cent is hospitality. What's more, these teas benefit from 'topping up'. Each almost-full cup or tumbler arrives with the dried leaves already unfurling to tender bright green tips in the near-boiling water, accompanied by a jug of hot water. Once the first

cupful is drunk, those same leaves will flavour several more. You may even eat the leaves if you like.

In ancient China tea was regarded as one of the seven daily necessities, and over the centuries tea has infiltrated every level of Chinese life. Workers and travellers carry flasks of it in convenient pouches, swinging from wrist straps. And while tea-bags and bottled tea are readily available, most locals prefer a steaming cup of the fresh brew.

'A cup of green tea, keeps three doctors away', is a common Chinese saying. And who would know better than them?

HANGZHOU LAKE PRAWNS WITH LONGJING TEA

500g (1lb) fresh prawns (shrimp) shelled
1 egg white, lightly beaten
2 teaspoons cornflour
1 teaspoon salt
2 cups (500ml/16fl oz) vegetable oil
1½ teaspoons chopped fresh ginger
2 teaspoons chopped green onion
2 teaspoons yellow rice wine
2 tablespoons freshly picked longjing tea leaves, OR
2-3 teaspoons 'white' tea leaves, steeped in ½ cup (125ml/4fl oz)
   boiling water

With a sharp knife, cut deeply along the centre back of each prawn to de-vein and butterfly.

In a dish combine the egg white, cornflour and salt and add the prepared prawn.

Mix well and leave for 10 minutes.

Heat the oil in a wok and when very hot add the shrimp and fry for about 30 seconds, until pink and firm. Remove with a slotted spoon and set aside.

Drain off the oil. Reheat the pan and when very hot return 1 tablespoon of the oil.

Add the ginger and onion and fry briefly. Return the shrimp and add the wine.

Drain most of the water from the tea leaves, tip leaves and remaining water over the shrimp and stir up.

Serve immediately.

WATER IN PARADISE

'LIVE IN HANGZHOU, MARRY IN SUZHOU, DINE IN GUANGZHOU AND DIE IN LUZHOU,' WE WERE TOLD WHEN WE VISITED THESE CITIES.

Of course we asked, 'why?' and the answer was: 'because these places have, respectively, the best view, the prettiest women, the best food and the best coffin wood!'

I can't say we confirmed the last one. We didn't make it to Luzhou which may have been just as well, although we did discover it is noted for its production of alcoholic drinks as well. The gastronomic delights of Guangzhou, a port on the Pearl River not far from Hong Kong, will have to wait for another time too.

The Chinese say, 'Above you have heaven, and below you have Hangzhou', meaning it is just that—a little piece of paradise to live in. We spent a happy couple of days visiting its various gardens, cruising on the West Lake and on into the hills to

a tea plantation. The Three Moon Reflection Island and the Pagoda of Six Harmonies, were so typically Chinese in both name and appearance, and then there was the street of teahouses, a real lifestyle option if ever I saw one.

Suzhou was different again with the chance to glide down the canals, past the locals' back gates, surprising old people relaxing, or waving to passengers in the other boats as we passed. The names of the many ancient public gardens were equally enticing: the Humble Administrator's Garden, the Lingering Garden, and the Master of Nets Garden, where musical items were delivered by appropriately pretty girls in pavilions scattered amongst them.

But one other town, not mentioned in the famous quotation, captured my imagination even more. Hong Cun was an artists' village surrounded by a lake. A true water village. Just newly opened to tourists, it is tranquil and unspoiled. Artists from all over the world have already discovered it and come here to paint the water-lily covered waters,

the steeply arched bridge, the walled village and the magical light.

In the centre of town women squatted, washing clothes in a large communal pool while beside them artists sat with their paints at the ready, dabbing away in sketchbooks or on easels. On the outside of the town the entire water's edge was lined by painters working on the scene in front of them in a hundred styles and dozens of interpretations. Yet the air of the place is not bohemian. It's more relaxed than that.

'Is it always busy like this?' I asked our guide.

'Oh, yes,' she replied, 'Groups of art students come to stay for a week or a month. Others come on day trips.'

So if I was to tamper with that famous adage about the towns, I'd have to add, 'relax in Hong Cun'.

BEGGAR'S CHICKEN

(ALSO KNOWN AS FORTUNE CHICKEN)

They say beggars in China invented this wonderfully fragrant chicken dish. They also say that at first the chicken was probably stolen and so had to be quickly hidden in mud and thrown into the fire both to avoid detection.

It was certainly a happy accident. Coating the chicken in mud, feathers and all, meant the bird cooked in its own juices. When it was baked and ready, the feathers came right off with the hardened crust.

Fast forward a couple of centuries and Beggar's Chicken has become classic Chinese haute cuisine without the mud. In both homes and restaurants, the mud pack has been substituted with a firm salt dough which also helps increase the heat and cooks the chicken quickly.

The liquid seasoning in this dish includes a potent Chinese wine, 'fen jiu'—an intensely aromatic clear liqueur which is almost gin-like in its perfume. It's expensive, but worth every cent when you crack the crust and the smell of the marinade rises.

1 large chicken (at least 2kg (4½lb)), dressed
2 cups chicken filling (see right)
A few pandan (screwpine) leaves, cut to 20cm (8in) lengths (substitute with banana leaves, or just leave out)
1 quantity salt dough (see right)

marinade

1 cup Chinese white wine (fen jiu) *
4 tablespoon light soy sauce
1 teaspoons five-spice powder
1 teaspoon black pepper, freshly cracked
1 teaspoon salt, 1 teaspoon sugar

* Substitute with a clear liqueur like Cointreau or a good gin, if you cannot get Chinese wine. Chinese wine is actually more liqueur than 'wine' so it's pretty strong.

Marinate the chicken: Combine ingredients for marinade into a bowl. Mix well. Rub chicken inside and out with the marinade. Put the bird in a large zip-lock bag or covered casserole and turn over occasionally. Leave for at least for an hour. Stuff chicken with filling. Close cavity with metal or bamboo skewers.

Place pandan leaves on a double layer of foil. Place bird on top of the leaves and wrap the foil tightly over. (The pandan leaves add fragrance and also prevents the chicken from sticking to the foil.)

Cook the chicken: Roll out dough and place foil wrapped chicken over dough. Bring up the sides of the dough to the TOP of the chicken. If you tuck dough ends UNDER chicken, you'll lose all the juices when you break open the chicken and serve. Pat dough down and prick with a fork to eliminate air pockets. Bake in very hot pre-heated 240°C (465°F) oven for 45 minutes. Turn oven down to 180°C (355°F) and continue cooking for another hour. Bring to table, break open crust and serve.

CHICKEN FILLING

1 tablespoon chopped back bacon
200g (7oz) belly pork, finely sliced
1 tablespoon minced ginger
1 brown onion, sliced very thinly
6 dried shiitake mushrooms, finely sliced
100g (3½oz) salted Sichuan pickled vegetable, sliced fine (optional)
1 carrot, diced
sesame oil, light soy sauce to taste
1 tablespoon Chinese wine, Shaoxing

Fry the chopped bacon and belly pork in a hot wok until oil from meat has separated. Add minced ginger and brown onion slices. Fry till fragrant. Add mushrooms and salted vegetables next. Add diced carrot and sesame oil, light soy sauce and Chinese wine and cook till filling gives off a pleasant aroma. Take filling off fire and allow to cool completely before stuffing the chicken.

SALT DOUGH

1kg (2¼lbs) plain flour
200g (7oz) rough salt or sea salt
Enough water to mix a firm dough

Place plain flour in a large mixing bowl. Mix in the salt. Make a depression in the middle of the flour and slowly mix in the water.

When the flour, salt and water mixture clumps and forms a dough, it's ready. (You can use the dough hook in your mixer if you want. But I find it very satisfying to dig my hands in and knead.)

Turn out the dough onto a floured board and knead with well-floured hands. When the dough feels elastic and is no longer too sticky, roll it out into a large rectangle.

Recipe © Pauline Loh, used with permission. www.cuisine-asia.com

SUNRISE ON YELLOW MOUNTAIN

WE WERE WOKEN UP AT 5AM BY OUR NEIGHBOURS' CHATTERING. THEY WERE MOVING AROUND NOISILY IN THE NEXT ROOM. I KNEW THEY WOULD BE PULLING ON HEAVY CLOTHES AND BIG BOOTS IN A HURRY.

The rush was on. Daybreak was at 5.45am, dawn at 6.15am. Too early for me and yet I couldn't stay in bed. The air of anticipation was infectious. Gordon was swiftly getting his camera gear together. He was not going to miss a moment of it either.

Peeping out through the windows I could see a thin line of brightness in the east and shadows scurrying around below in the forecourt. Soon streams of people in red caps and warmly padded maroon jackets lent to them by the hotel were heading for the paths that led to the lookouts. Already I could see a bright cluster on a high ridge and hear the shouts and whoops of some people, as if encouraging the sun to rise. The Yellow Mountains are really 72 peaks in the space of 1200 square kilometres near Tunxi, south-west of Shanghai.

While they have been known and revered for centuries, only recently have western tourists been encouraged and catered for. I had been unsure of what to expect. The little information I could find before leaving home spoke of difficult climbs just to reach the hotel itself. There was a cable car which ruled out several hours of climbing, but what then? And what about our luggage? Our travel company suggested taking just the bare essentials, so we did.

As it turned out, the cable car deposited us above the hotel at 1730 metres (5675 feet) allowing us to walk the last 450 steps down to it quite easily. More arduous was the hike to the summit of Mount Huangshan, but it too was on a well made path.

Those who cannot physically do this have the option of hiring porters with sedan chairs. These men are used to such loads. I watched in awe one day as several passed me on a path, each carrying hefty rocks at either end of a bamboo pole. Every rock, tile and brick of the hotels (there are two in this area) had to be transported this way. Even now garbage, laundry and supplies are carried in and out by porter.

In a typically Chinese way, the attractions of the Yellow Mountains are listed and numbered. There are four 'wonders': odd-shaped pines, grotesque rock formations, seas of constantly changing clouds, and crystal-clear springs. Daybreak is the ideal time to see at least three of these.

With moments to go, the tall finger-shaped peaks which look lifted from a Chinese scroll painting were still snuggled in the downy clouds that swirled and reformed instantly around them. I watched for a while as the nearest peak sank in the mist. It had been an island just moments ago. I had the sensation that I was flying over the clouds.

Then the sun rose on time, thrusting spikes of light into the eyes of the onlookers, and sending the photographers mad with excitement. Those twisted ancient pines clung tenaciously to the precipitous rock faces as suddenly the mountains assumed substance and reared clear of the mist as if reaching for the sunshine.

CRISPY SKIN FISH WITH SWEET AND SOUR SAUCE

This is a special dish as it looks so glamorous and colourful.

750g (1½lbs) whole snapper, cleaned and scaled, but with head and tail left on
½ teaspoon salt
½ teaspoon five spice powder

SWEET AND SOUR SAUCE

1 carrot, thinly sliced
3 tablespoons frozen or fresh peas
1 tablespoon light soy sauce
1 tablespoon mirin
3 tablespoons tomato sauce or puree
2 tablespoons vinegar
2 tablespoons sugar or honey
¾ cup (180ml/6fl oz) water
1 tablespoon cornflour
3 tablespoons cold water
2 tablespoons peanut oil
2 cloves garlic, crushed
½ teaspoon finely grated fresh ginger
1 small onion, cut in wedges
2 tablespoons mango, sliced (optional)

oil to fry
1 egg, beaten
¼ cup cornflour or kudzu

Wash fish well and wipe dry. Slash skin diagonally on each side, several times in opposite directions to make diamond shapes.

Mix salt and five spice powder together and rub into fish skin and slashes.

To make the sauce, bring a little water to the boil, then add carrots and peas. Cook one minute, drain, then drop into cold water. Set aside.

Combine soy sauce, mirin, tomato sauce or puree, vinegar, sugar or honey and water and stir to dissolve sugar. Mix cornflour with the cold water. Heat oil and add garlic, ginger, peas, carrots and onion. Fry for 2 minutes.

Add sauce mixture, bring to the boil, then carefully add dissolved cornflour. Stir until thickened, then add mango if using. Keep warm while frying fish. Heat oil in a large frypan, large enough for the fish, and deep enough so there is no splattering of oil. Dip fish in egg then cornflour. Fry fish for approximately 4 minutes on each side, or until cooked through. Drain, place on a serving platter and spoon a little sauce over.

Accompany with a bowl of sauce served separately.

SERVES 4

green. We had seen factories dumping refuse into a river earlier in the day and wondered if there was a connection, but realised we could never know for sure. It was hot and much of time we had to keep the windows closed in the bus because of the car exhausts and dusty roads. The driver kept the aircon off, too, because his bus needed its power to get up the hills, especially the last pass just before Dali. We passed children swimming and splashing in rivers and lakes and envied them.

It is a stunning trip, starting with deep woods of fir trees and ending in a magnificent plain on the eastern side of the pass.

The soil in this part of Yunnan is rich and red and sometimes almost a purplish colour—a rusty colour, as there is probably iron in the soil. The rice paddies and terraces were scalloped, much like receding wave patterns on the sea shore.

'CROSSING THE BRIDGE' NOODLES

1 kg (2¼lb) chicken necks and bones, for stock
10-12 cups
1 green onion
2cm (¾in) piece fresh ginger
1 star anise (optional)
400g (14oz) fresh egg noodles
125g chicken breast
100g (3½oz) boneless white fish
100g (3½oz) small shelled prawns
60g (2oz) baby spinach or bok choy leaves
1 tablespoon rice wine
1 tablespoon light soy sauce
6 thin slices fresh ginger
salt to taste
2 tablespoons rendered chicken fat

To make the stock for the soup-noodles, rinse the chicken necks and bones and drain well. Place in a large pot and add the water, green onion and star anise. Bring to the boil, then reduce heat and simmer gently for about 1 hour, skimming frequently.

Remove from the heat and strain into a clean saucepan. Set aside to cool, and when cold skim off the fat and set aside. Return the stock to the heat and simmer until reduced to a half of its original volume.

To cook the noodles, bring a pan of lightly salted water to the boil and simmer noodles for about 1½ minutes. Drain and transfer to a deep bowl and cover to keep warm.

Very thinly slice the chicken and fish. Place the uncooked chicken fish, prawns and spinach on the noodles.

Into the hot, reduced stock add the wine, soy sauce and ginger, adding salt to taste. Stir in the chicken fat and pour over the noodles and raw meats. Stir with chopsticks.

Serve into deep soup bowls.

SERVES 4-6

Recipe © Jacki Passmore, used with permission

CHOCOLATE GINGER LYCHEES

Lychees are wonderful on their own, but this is the best and most decadent way to enjoy them. It is probably not an old Chinese recipe, but it is worth including.

1 can lychees, drained and patted dry
   or 16 fresh lychees, peeled and seed removed
16 pieces of crystallised ginger cut to fill the cavity of each lychee
375g (12oz) dark chocolate, melted

Line a baking tray with kitchen paper. Make sure that the lychees are not damp as the chocolate will not cover them properly. Stuff the cavities with ginger then, using a fork or tongs, carefully dip each one in the chocolate, swirling to cover completely. Place on the kitchen paper to set. When all the lychees are done, place the tray in a cool place (preferably not the refrigerator) until hardened completely. Serve as an after-dinner treat or with coffee.

GINGER

GINGER COMES FROM THE SAME
FAMILY AS CARDAMON, GALANGAL
AND TURMERIC, AND IS REFERRED TO
AS FRESH, GREEN OR ROOT GINGER.

Once half of all Oriental prescriptions included ginger, yet today you're more likely to find it in many Chinese dishes, buried deep at the beginning of a stir-fry so that its fragrant flavour seeps through everything, or finely sliced and scattered fresh along with coriander and other aromatic herbs for example on top of a deep-fried whole fish.

Ginger has been preserved for centuries in China, often crystallised, which is how glacé ginger entered British cookery some time ago.

The Chinese believe ginger is useful for a range of diseases: all sorts of stomach upsets, as well as rheumatoid arthritis, osteoarthritis, migraines, or upper respiratory tract infections. Some Chinese practitioners would prescribe fresh ginger to treat acute bacterial dysentery and snake bite, yet it is also said to alleviate toothache and help with baldness. Women customarily are advised to drink a mixture of ginger cooked in wine and sesame oil shortly after giving birth. And, yes, there is a Chinese version of Chicken Soup, that panacea for all ills, but it is redolent of ginger too.

I first tried Cheuk at breakfast, because it appears everywhere in China and is really a congee, a sort of rice gruel laced with shreds of chicken and finely grated fresh ginger. It came topped with thick slices of deep-fried garlic and accompanied by a thousand-year-old egg with a mottled grey shell which I couldn't quite bring myself to crack open— even though I knew it was only more like 100 DAYS old. As I watched the other diners breaking theirs apart I was even more sure I did not want to eat it. The inside was discoloured and strange-looking, the white greyish and almost transparent.

The soup itself was joy enough and I dipped into it pieces of the fried bread which had also been brought to go with it. Really, I suppose it was quite bland yet I could feel its goodness in every spoonful. I badgered the chef until he scribbled down the ingredients for me and even now, back at home, if we feel a virus coming on I make a big pot of this and immediately begin to feel better.

INTO THE SCROLL PAINTING

THE AMAZING LANDSCAPES OF GUILIN, IN GUANXI PROVINCE, ARE ONE THING— AND PERHAPS THE THING THAT DRAWS MOST TOURISTS. CERTAINLY I THOUGHT THAT AS WE CHUG-A-LUGGED ALONG THE TRANQUIL JADE-GREEN LI RIVER AS PART OF A CAVALCADE OF HOOTING BOATS, THEIR TOURIST GUIDE COMMENTARIES BOOMING.

Most westerners would recognise pictures of the unusual limestone karst formations and peaks of this region which were thrust up 300 million years ago. It looks just as if a giant has dropped a green and blue sheet over a crowd of people, who stand like a cast waiting for their cue to move on-stage (see the picture on page 91).

The Li River is sold as 'a hundred miles of river, a hundred miles of picture galleries'. It is certainly majestic country, with mountains thrusting up like stony fingers in all directions. But it is not all tourism. On the water we passed people in small boats snacking on bowls of something, and others washing clothes on the river's edge, ducks and ducklings, and the occasional bamboo raft.

In the stern of our boat, close enough to the water that they could toss the scraps overboard, a group of cooks squatted preparing our meal. They didn't looked at all fussed, working smoothly and swiftly, even though they had a crowded boatload of tourists to cater for.

It all made sense later when I discovered that Guilin has a proud history in the culinary field. The area is known for the fermented bean curd developed over 300 years ago, and said to be the best of its kind in China.

Guilin rice noodles (especially when boiled in a soup of horse bones, the locals say) and served topped with cured and deep fried horsemeat is another specialty. No doubt you will also be advised to wash this down with the local thrice-brewed Sanhua alcohol. This liquor features as an ingredient, along with lobster sauce and garlic, in the fragrant local red pepper sauce.

Follow all this with a dessert of Guilin lychees, said to be the sweetest and the best in the country, fresh pomelos (a sort of tropical grapefruit) or mangosteens, and you will begin to understand this region's claims in the kitchen.

Lychees (sometimes spelled litchee, litchi or lichee) are rich in vitamin C. Their ultra-sweetness makes them ideal for desserts although they are sometimes used in Chinese cookery with poultry and savoury dishes.

Doubtless it was to this region that courtiers of an empress in the Tang dynasty (618–907AD) were dispatched. Luckily for her, people in that luxury-loving era admired plump women as that well-endowed lady was said to crave lychees and indulged in as many as three hundred a day.

99

LOBSTER IN GINGER SAUCE

MARINADE

1 tablespoon egg white (lightly beaten)
salt
white pepper
1 tablespoon cornflour
1 lobster tail

3 cups (750ml/24fl oz) of peanut oil (for frying)
20g (¾oz) fresh ginger, cut in thick slices
15g (½oz) spring onions (shallots, scallions) cut in
    5cm (2in) (use the white part)
good pinch of salt
pinch of pepper
½ teaspoon sugar
2 teaspoons Shaoxing wine (Chinese rice wine)
½ teaspoon light soy sauce
chicken stock
1 teaspoon corn flour mixed in a little cold water
    or stock to thicken

Marinate the lobster: Mix all the marinade ingredients together. Set aside. Cut the lobster tail through the shell into good bite sized pieces. Mix with the marinade and leave for 5–10 minutes.

Heat the peanut oil in a hot wok until the oil is smoking, then reduce to a medium heat. Add the lobster pieces and fry in the hot oil for one minute. Remove the lobster with a slotted spoon, drain and put to one side. Drain and reserve the oil from the wok, and wipe the wok clean.

Put two tablespoons of the oil back into the wok, heat and fry the ginger and spring onions for 30 seconds. Return the lobster to the wok and stir-fry over a high heat for another few seconds.

Add the salt, pepper, sugar, soy and wine and continue to stir-fry quickly. Add the chicken stock, cover with the wok lid, and simmer for a minute. Stir in the cornflour, thickening until the lobster pieces are glazed. Serve immediately.

SERVES 2

Recipe © Ping Yan Yeung, Chef de Cuisine, Silks, Crown Towers, Melbourne., used with permission. www.silk@crowntowers.com.au.

CHINESE GOOSEBERRIES

I AM SURE THE EMPRESS WOULD HAVE APPLAUDED THIS SWEETMEAT.

Kiwi fruit should rightfully be called Chinese gooseberries or 'yangtao', as the Chinese themselves call them.

Over 400 varieties of this soft and furry egg-shaped fruit have been grown in China for over seven centuries and more recently exported to most other countries. However it took some enterprising New Zealanders in 1962 to rename them 'kiwi fruit', export them to the US, and corner an entire market.

Kiwi fruit is a good source of potassium and chromium which is said to be useful in the management of diabetes. Eat one and you also get almost all the vitamin C you need for a day.

Chinese gooseberries were first discovered in the Yangtse river valley where they grew wild on vines wrapped around trees. The court of the great Khans were understandably partial to their flavour, texture and colour—all the things that still win them fans today.

Cultivation of this fruit began in the 17th century in China. A collector for the Royal Horticultural Society of Britain in the 19th century sent some samples to England, and later cuttings of the vines were taken to the US. The word was out.

Dessert in China is usually very low-key in any case. Often it is simply some fresh fruit—unadorned slices of apples, oranges, nashi pear or melon—served as a perfunctory afterthought to a banquet.

I have never encountered this most Chinese of fruits in season there. I am sure in the right regions at the right time, they make a welcome appearance.

FUNGUS POWER

MUSHROOMS HAVE LONG BEEN ASSOCIATED WITH HEALTH AND LONG LIFE. INDEED, CARVINGS OF THE TAOIST GOD OF LONGEVITY, SHOULAU, OFTEN FEATURE A MUSHROOM.

While mushrooms are native to China and have been cultivated for well over 1000 years (some say over 6000 years), the most popular fungus—and they use a lot in China—is the shiitake.

In China, workers packing shiitake mushrooms have been found to live longer and suffer fewer respiratory complaints. The name we use today is the Japanese word. In English they may be called Chinese black mushrooms.

A physician from the Ming Dynasty (1368–1644 A.D.) is recorded as advising that these mushrooms were also useful for treating upper respiratory diseases, poor blood circulation, liver trouble, exhaustion and weakness, and as a tonic for overall well-being. Perhaps now we know why. An active compound called lentinan has been discovered in these mushrooms, and credited with many of the same benefits the good doctor attributed so long ago, mainly because of its assistance to our immune systems. This has great implications for fighting infections and diseases such as the flu and other viruses, and for people with an impaired immune system such as those living with AIDS.

Shiitake mushrooms are available fresh or dried, but invariably the stems are very tough and should be discarded or else simmered with a little water to provide a mushroom stock. When using dried mushrooms, always soak them before cooking them.

They add a subtle flavour to stir-fries and claypot dishes and their firm, meaty texture makes them a good addition to vegetarian recipes. Many Chinese prefer sun-dried shiitakes to the fresh because they say they develop a distinct and more savoury aroma during the drying process.

HAKKA MEAT ROLL

The Hakka meat roll is a must-have dish during the first day of the Lunar New Year celebrations. In the past, the meat roll was wrapped in pork caul, a lacy fatty membrane that encases the internal organs of the pig. My mum would often have to pre-order the pork caul from the butcher at least a month ahead. These days, due to health reasons, she has substituted it with bean curd sheet.

But once a year, during the reunion dinner, we still get to eat the meat roll in the traditional way: Wrapped in sinful pork caul and pan fried over low heat till the fat is melted away and fused with the meat roll.

250g (8oz) minced fatty pork
200g (6½oz) tiger prawns, deveined, shelled
    and cut into 4 sections
10 pieces of diced water chestnuts
1 egg
1 teaspoon ground white pepper
2 tablespoons fish sauce
1 teaspoon sesame oil
1 teaspoon rice wine
1 piece bean curd sheet

   In a mixing bowl, mix all the ingredients together except the bean curd sheet.
   Cut bean curd sheet into rectangles measuring 15 x 10cm (6 inches by 4 inches). Wipe the beancurd sheet with a damp cloth to wet the surface so that it will be easier to roll and seal.
   Scoop 3–4 tablespoons of the mixture on each sheet and roll up.
   Steam over high heat for 5 minutes. Remove from steamer.
   Heat oil in frying pan with cooking oil and pan fry each roll till it's golden brown.
   Drain on paper towels and cut into smaller sections. Serve with chilli sauce.

Recipe © Gina Choong, used with permission. www.kitchencapers.net

THE GRAIN
THAT FEEDS
A NATION

IN DALI WE SAW RICE IN PADDY FIELDS BESIDE THE ROAD. THERE WERE SUNFLOWERS TOO, GIANT ONES WITH CENTRES AS BIG AS BREAD AND BUTTER PLATES PACKED FULL OF SPIRAL ROWS OF DARK SEEDS.

We could see too how the farmers collected the rice, first into stooks, then stacked these on top of each other into pagoda shaped stacks. The process seemed to be that women were responsible for planting the seed then cutting it with heavy scythes. The men fed the cut rice stalks into a thresher, some pedal driven, others with a motor, right in the field. The women then took the threshed stalks and tied them in bundles which they arranged into stooks and

finally haystacks. Ultimately, we were told, this hay is used as the binder in adobe bricks, or as stock feed, or burned and the ash used as a fertiliser.

After the grain is threshed, the whole lot is put into bags (by women of course) and then carted off to be winnowed—we passed many groups almost enveloped in fine chaffy dust as they did this—and ultimately spread out to dry on concrete slabs.

Chillies and corn are dried that way too, and we became used to finding red or yellow or grey-white pools of drying produce on footpaths and open areas, including roads from time to time, although the tobacco we saw was mostly hung over poles.

On the rice terraces, scalloping upwards to the tops of the hills, the ripening golden rice contrasted against the green of the stalks and the blue sky and misty air. It made it harder to realise that this region was not just about

postcard pictures. Intense, back-breakingly hard work by everyone is needed to grow and harvest a grain on which the lives of millions depend.

As we drove, we saw rice, then corn and sunflowers and finally tobacco started to make an appearance. Later we saw buckwheat in the distance, draped white and flowery on the hillsides.

Once we reached higher ground, even more tobacco was being grown on terraces, and we were told that the people from the mountain areas smoke a lot because the effects goes through their skin and the smell is said to scare away the snakes.

Steamed white rice always almost always accompanies a meal in China, although often appearing later in the meal. The general belief is that the first part of the meal should be enough to satisfy the diner, but should there be any room left, the rice will make sure everyone is well fed.

The Mandarin word 'fan' refers to both 'rice' and 'food' so a courteous enquiry is 'Have you eaten rice (food) yet?'

HAKKA YONG TAU FOO

STUFFING

300g (10oz) minced threadfin fish
500g (1lb) minced lean pork
100g (3½oz) minced fatty pork
60g (2oz) salted fish, minced
100g (3½oz) dried shrimps, soaked and chopped
300g (10oz) bamboo shoots
10 water chestnuts, peeled and diced

SEASONING

1½ teaspoons salt
2 teaspoons fish sauce
2 teaspoons light soy sauce
2 teaspoons sugar

1 bitter gourd, seeded and cut into rings
5 dried mushrooms (soaked)
2 green and 2 red chillis
1 red and 1 yellow capsicum (bell pepper), cut into quarters and seeded
3 tablespoons cornflour
1 beaten egg
2 pieces bean curd, cut into half
5 pieces tau pok (bean puffs), cut into half

SOUP

200g (7oz) ikan bilis, fried and pounded
100g (3½oz) soy beans
6 cups (1.5 litres) of water

To make the stuffing: shred bamboo shoots and set aside. In a mixing bowl, mix all remaining stuffing ingredients. Add bamboo shoots and seasoning mixture and knead mixture to mix. Set aside.

Dust surface of gourd, mushrooms, chillis and capsicum with a little cornflour. Stuff with meat mixture and coat with beaten egg.

Scoop out centre of bean curd to make a cavity and stuff.

Make soup by heating up water in a large pot to boil. Add soy beans and simmer and cook for 1 hour.

Finally add pounded ikan bilis, stir to mix and cook for another 10 minutes. Blanch each stuffed vegetable in the hot soup to briefly cook it. Drain and remove. Heat up cooking oil and pan fry vegetables.

Serve with rice or noodles with soup by the side.

Recipe © Gina Choong, used with permission, www.kitchencapers.net

SERVES 6-8

WOK WORK

WHEREVER YOU TRAVEL IN CHINA, YOU ARE NEVER FAR FROM A WOK.

When you think about it they are an amazingly versatile and useful piece of kitchen equipment. Common in China for at least 3000 years, they were originally designed to for use over primitive wood or charcoal fires. A wok's small base means it can be used over a small flame or fire, yet the sloping sides allow large quantities of food to be tossed and stirred with ease.

Woks are not only ideal for stir-frying. Place two chopsticks across the inside and balance a steamer or plate on them to cook food more gently. The wok may also be used for poaching, deep frying, stewing or simmering, or even to smoke food.

The shape of woks varies between the north where pans have two handles, one on each side, and the south of China, where they feature one longer handle, like a frypan.

The Chinese say they like to sit near the kitchen, because it is from this vantage point they 'get the breath of the wok'. Certainly this quick method of cooking prevents the loss of vitamins that are destroyed by prolonged high heat. Steaming, commonly done in bamboo steamers, often stacked several layers high on top of a wok half-filled with bubbling water, also preserves nutrients.

WOK TIPS

Most Asian supply stores stock cheaper woks than gourmet kitchen shops or department stores. Try to buy a few different sizes for large and small dishes. If you use gas, also buy a stabilising ring for the pan. Woks will work on electric hotplates, but seem to perform best with gas. A wok with a frypan-handle

on one side is good—it's even better if there is a small handle on the opposite side, because a wok full of hot food can sometimes be heavy to manipulate one-handed.

Before using your wok for the first time, wash it well with hot soapy water. Make this the last time you ever wash it. Dry it, then wipe oil all over the inside and outside. Place it over a high heat and let it burn off the oil for ten or more minutes. Wipe off all the excess burned oil with a paper kitchen towel, then store in a dry place. After each use, wipe out or rinse very lightly, then dry. Initially, rub a light film of oil over the wok before putting it away, but after prolonged use, there will be a build-up of 'seasoning' and you should not need to continue to oil it.

Before cooking, place some oil in the base of the pan and let it get quite hot. Always cook over a high heat. Because cooking time is so quick, make sure that all ingredients are prepared beforehand and do not leave the wok. You should be free to lift and turn the food the whole time so that it cooks evenly.

When adding liquids, pour them down the side of the pan so that they heat as they run in and don't form a pool of cooler liquid in the base. It is essential that the food stays at an even heat as it can begin to steam—that's when vegetables will lose their characteristic crunchy-crisp texture.

Always add the longest-cooking foods first—onions, carrot, capsicum, celery—and finish with foods that need the least—snow peas, green onions, bean sprouts and mushrooms. Add new ingredients by clearing a space in the base where they may heat quickly, while the food on the sides stays warm without further cooking.

WILTED LETTUCE AND CUCUMBER STIR-FRY

This dish creates surprising flavours, textures and aromas. This recipe was cooked for me by my Cantonese Amah and makes a wonderful stir-fry. Chinese melon or 'sinqua' may be peeled sliced and used instead of cucumber.

½ tablespoon vegetable oil
2 cloves garlic, crushed or chopped finely
3 cucumbers, seeded then sliced into finger widths
1 red capsicum (bell pepper), seeded, membrane removed, sliced
1 lettuce, washed and shaken dry then chopped coarsely
3cm (1¼in) ginger, pounded to release the juice
¼ cup (60ml/2fl oz) black Chinese dark vinegar
1 tablespoon Xiao Xing wine
2 teaspoons plum sauce (if necessary)

Heat a wok until it smokes, add oil and lower heat, testing heat with a skewer, the oil should bubble around its pointed end.

Fry garlic until golden only for a few seconds, add cucumber and capsicum, sweat slightly. Add lettuce, allow to sweat, covered for 1 minute then add ginger juice and sauces.

Toss well working quickly season to taste with sufficient sweet sour chilli and tart flavours which should be balanced perfectly.

(You will gradually become adept at this balance of flavours as your palate adapts to Asian tastes.)

Serve immediately with hot rice and braised fish as a main dish.

SERVES 4–6 WITH RICE

Recipe © Carol Selva Rajah, used with permission

TEA FOR TWO BILLION

Tea accompanies every Chinese meal, and people frequently passed us in the street swinging flasks of green tea as they headed off to work.

In fact the Chinese have used tea in medicine for 4000 years referring first to it in 350AD, but it did not arrive in Japan until 850AD, and in Europe even later via the Dutch East India Co in 1609.

At Meijiawu village near Hangzhou, south-west of Shanghai, we visited the Dragon Well tea plantation, gently fingering the delicate tips on the low bushes, then watching as freshly picked leaves were hand-dried nearby. It was a tedious and hot task for the man who used his bare hands to swirl the leaves in a wok-like dish with a little white tea oil. After eight hours his job was done, the leaves crisped to perfection. The result? One kilogram (2lb) of fresh leaves had produced just 125 grams (4oz) of this tea, regarded as one of the finest in China.

LITTLE WONDER A POPULAR CHINESE SAYING GOES: 'BETTER TO BE DEPRIVED OF FOOD FOR THREE DAYS, THAN TEA FOR ONE'.

Picking is just as painstaking. Only girls are employed to pick the leaves by hand and it takes each one ten hours to gather two kilos (4lb).

In the tasting room we tasted and sniffed teas harvested in April and May, learning that the northern spring produces premier shoots. The difference was quite clear. A tray of lesser tea brought for our education, tasted like mown grass while the better grade had a nutty toastiness to it.

As we left, we noticed in the courtyard a statue of Luxu, the seventh-century 'tea sage', the first person to write a book about tea.

Some teahouses offer food; many include it in the price of the tea. The Little Art House, in the aptly-named Tea House Street (Shuguang Road), in the southern city of Hangzhou, has a small room crammed with every delicacy available: earthenware pots on burners holding soups, corn cobs and noodles; blue pottery jars of nuts and seeds and dried fruits, and dishes of fruit and salad vegetables. Pay 100–150 yuan, and you are welcome to stay and eat and drink tea, seated in bamboo-lined cubicles all day if you wish.

Called 'queen of the camellias' tea was supposedly discovered when some dried 'camellia thea' leaves fell into the cauldron of Emperor Shen Nung of China in 2737BC. He was delighted that it helped him stay awake and tea became synonymous with China from then on.

Another legend says that it originated from the torn-off eyelids of a Buddhist saint who maimed himself because he fell asleep after two years of sleepless meditating. While that may seem an incredible feat, he was disappointed because he had planned on ten!

Long ago tea-clippers raced from China to England with their precious cargoes and excited national interest. China's wealth of culture, gathered over thousands of years, celebrates this basic necessity of life. Little wonder a popular Chinese saying goes: 'Better to be deprived of food for three days, than tea for one'.

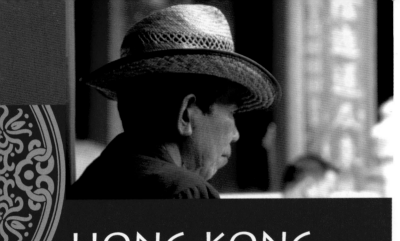

HONG KONG CUISINE

IT'S NOT SURPRISING THAT HONG KONG'S FOOD HAS DEVELOPED IN MUCH THE SAME WAY AS THE CITY.

On the one hand it is a vibrant, cosmopolitan metropolis, the perfect blend between east and west. There are gleaming modern buildings and fine hotels, yet the ancient beliefs are only a breath away, for no architect or engineer would consider sanctioning a new building for which 'feng shui' had not been consulted.

So it is with the food. Trendy bars cater to urban business people and smart cafés and restaurants serve a range of Asian and fusion dishes. At home most tables still feature the local and immensely varied Cantonese dishes, as well as Hakka food and some that lean more towards Shanghai.

Dim sum dishes are popular for breakfast and at other times during the day at teahouses throughout the city because people can order as much or as little as they want. This is 'yum cha', which means, literally, 'drinking tea'. This practice is common throughout all of the southern region and has spread to other parts of China and overseas.

Its island location makes Hong Kong the ideal place for seafood restaurants serving absolutely the freshest fish. This is ensured by allowing diners to select the exact fish or crustacean they wish to eat from a tank. Seafood such as lobster and abalone are greatly prized on the island, although there is one famous restaurant in Hong Kong which is noted for the roast goose it serves.

Perhaps more than in any other city in China, visitors to Hong Kond can be readily exposed to most of the country's varied cuisines. Its multicultural and urbane professional population accepts and glories in this, and is more than ready to show it off to the world.

SEVEN FACTS ABOUT HONG KONG

1 The Central-Mid-Levels Escalator and Walkway System in Hong Kong is an important transport link between Des Voeux Road in Central with Conduit Road in the Mid-levels. Completed in 1993, it is the world's longest covered escalator system, according to Guinness World Records. It is an amazing 800 metre (half a mile) combination of escalators and covered walkways with 20 reversible one-way escalators and three travelators, and the capacity to accommodate 210,600 passengers a day. A dining precinct, known as Soho, has been built around the Escalator with many restaurants and bars on Elgin and Staunton Streets.

2 In 2000, Hong Kong ranked as the fourth largest film producing economy behind India, the US and Japan. In terms of per capita production, Hong Kong is first in the world.

HONG KONG WAS THE FIRST CITY IN THE WORLD TO SET UP AN INDEPENDENT COMMISSION TO COMBAT CORRUPTION.

3 You can join a dolphin discovery cruise and hope to see the endangered Chinese white dolphin at play. Cruises depart Queen's Pier on Hong Kong Island.

4 The Hong Kong Jockey Club is entered in the Guinness World Records as the world's biggest non-profit racing club. Revenue from betting enables the Jockey Club to sponsor charity programs. In 2000/01 the Hong Kong Jockey Club Charities Trust donated HK$1.064 billion (US$136.4 million) to 180 charities and community projects.

5 Kowloon means 'nine dragons' and was named in the 13th century for its eight hills. Eight? The ninth 'dragon' was a piece of flattery for the thirteenth century emperor who was complimented that he was seen as a dragon too. The last of the Sung dynasty, he was a ten year old boy at the time.

6 The world's tallest outdoor seated bronze Buddha statue sits on the hillside of Ngong Ping on Lantau Island. The Statue is 26 metres (85 feet) tall and weighs 202 tonnes. The project took 10 years to complete and was unveiled in 1993.

7 Hong Kong was the first city in the world to set up an independent commission to combat corruption. .

CHICKEN-FILLED SHIITAKE MUSHROOMS

32 large Chinese black (shiitake) mushrooms, soaked for
30 minutes in hot water, drained and stems discarded
1 cup chicken mince
½ teaspoon shrimp paste
1 small onion, chopped
1 tablespoon cornflour
1 egg
1 tablespoon each soy sauce and mirin

SAUCE

1 cup (250ml/8fl oz) chicken stock
1 tablespoon cornflour
1 teaspoon sesame seed oil
1 teaspoon soy sauce

Match mushrooms into equal-sized pairs. Mix chicken mince, shrimp paste, onion, cornflour, egg, mirin and soy sauce in a bowl. Mound one tablespoonful into the caps of half the mushrooms. Top with remaining mushrooms. Press well together. Steam 20–30 minutes. Make sauce by dissolving cornflour in a little chicken stock. Set aside. Heat remaining stock and other ingredients until boiling. Stir in dissolved cornflour and cook, stirring, until thickened. Pour over mushrooms and serve very hot.

MAKES 16

PORTUGUESE TARTS

The key to this is rolling the pastry so it allows the flaky layers to show around the edge, and also cooking the tarts at a high heat.

3 egg yolks
½ cup caster sugar
2 tablespoons cornflour
1 cup (250ml/8fl oz) cream
½ cup (125ml/4fl oz) water
1 teaspoon grated lemon zest
2 teaspoons vanilla essence
1 sheet puff pastry, thawed

Whisk egg yolks, cornflour and sugar together in a bowl, then pour into a small saucepan set over a medium heat. Stir well, then slowly add cream and water, mixing until smooth. Add lemon zest, then heat just until the mixture boils. Remove immediately from the heat, stir in vanilla, and set aside to cool.

Tightly roll the sheet of pastry from the short side, then cut the rolled up pastry into 12 rounds. Lay rounds, cut-side up on a board and roll out each one into a 10cm (8in) circle. Press each circle into a muffin hole in a well-greased 12-hole pan. Strain custard and spoon enough into each pastry case to almost fill it. Bake in a preheated 220°C (430°F) oven for 20 minutes or until tops are blistered and very well-browned. Remove from trays and cool on racks.

MAKES 12

HOW NOW MACAU?

THE JETFOIL CONNECTION FROM HONG KONG TO MACAU TAKES JUST ONE HOUR. IF I'D BEEN VERY RICH I COULD EVEN HAVE COME BY HELICOPTER.

Macau is not simply an extension of Hong Kong. It is very definitely its own place, with a personality that has evolved over centuries—first Chinese, then Portuguese and now a blend of cultures: traders, manufacturers, missionaries and migrants—who have drifted ashore throughout its long history.

Macau had been Europe's oldest colony in China, its connection dating back to the 16th century. Portugal handed it back to China in 1999, just two years after Britain's handover of Hong Kong, and Macau is now a Special Administrative Region like Hong Kong. Many people equate Macau with its more glitzy enterprises—the casinos, an annual Grand Prix, as well as horse and greyhound racing—which have won it international attention.

While these are of major importance to tourism and the local economy, I was glad I made time to check out the sleepy island villages linked by causeways to the south, the shops filled with Chinese antiques, jewellery and gold, and of course the food.

With such a multi-cultural heritage, Macau's cuisine has to be one of the most complex in China. Everyone has heard of those Portuguese-style custard tarts, but there is so much more here. Many dishes have entered the Macanese repertoire from Brazil, India and Africa because of Portuguese settlements in those countries. Combine these with dishes from southern China and you have a magnificent blend of flavours and techniques, often quite fiery and exotic.

With its coastal position, of course seafood features in many dishes, as well as 'bacalhau', that favourite dried fish from Portugal. Another benefit of its European heritage is that Portuguese wines are affordable and available here too.

In Macau, you need two or three days, I discovered, just to whip around the major tourist spots—the soaring 338-metre (1108 feet) Macau Tower, the Ecumenical Centre, topped by a controversial twenty-metre bronze statue, the imposing grey 17th-century facade of St Paul's church, and of course the place everyone recognises in photographs: the main Senate Square, paved with those distinctive swirling wavelike tile patterns. Finally, with those must-dos ticked off, I made sure I reserved a little time to kick back and absorb the feel of Macau. And what better place than in a café with a strong coffee and a custard tart?

MANGO PUDDING
(PUDIM DE MANGO)

flesh of 6 mangoes, cubed
½ cup (100ml/4fl oz) cream
2 cups (500ml/16fl oz) milk
500g (1lb) sugar
45g (1¾oz) gelatine
6 cups (1.5litres/2½pts) water

  Place mango cubes into the base of individual pudding moulds
or one large serving dish. Mix together cream and milk. Boil sugar,
gelatine and water until dissolved, cool to room temperature then pour
gently into the milk mixture. Stir well and pour into the moulds or serving
dish. Chill for several hours, until firm.

SERVES 10

Recipe © Macau Government Tourist Office, used with permission..

CODFISH SOUP MACANESE (SOPA DE BACALHAU À MACAENSE)

'Bacalhau' (cod fish) is a staple ingredient in Portuguese and Macanese dishes. It needs to be soaked for around 24 hours, changing the water several times before use. You will find it in most Portuguese supermarkets.

160g (5½oz) soaked codfish
140g (5oz) cooked pork meat
60g (2oz) cornflour
1 teaspoon sugar
1 teaspoon sesame oil
1 tablespoon dark soy sauce
salt and pepper to taste
½ cup Chinese wine
1 tablespoon chicken stock powder
4½ cups (1.1litres/2.3pts) codfish stock
80g (2¾oz) rice vermicelli
1 tablespoon cornflour
2 egg whites, lightly beaten
few sprigs fresh coriander (cilantro), finely chopped
¼ cup chopped chives

   Remove the fish bone from the codfish and shred the flesh. Shred the pork meat and marinate for 15 minutes with the fish with the first quantity of cornflour, sugar, sesame oil, soy sauce, wine, salt and pepper. Meanwhile blend the fish and chicken stocks with chicken stock powder and adjust the flavour to taste. Add the marinated fish and pork and bring to the boil. Soak vermicelli in cold water until soft, then add to the soup. Mix cornflour with a little cold water and add to thicken the soup. Remove the soup from the heat and whisk in the egg whites. Sprinkle with coriander and chives to serve.

SERVES 10

DEEP FRIED PORK PIES

CHILICOTES

1 tablespoon corn oil
1 chopped onion
1 clove garlic, minced
1 teaspoon turmeric
100g (3½oz) minced pork
1 small potato, chopped
flour
salt and pepper to taste
1 egg yolk, lightly beaten

PASTRY

160g (6oz) flour
40ml water
1 teaspoon salt
2 egg
4 tablespoons vegetable oil

To make the stuffing: Place onion and garlic in a frying pan with corn oil and stir fry until tender. Add turmeric and pork and cook, stirring, until done. Add chopped potatoes and seasoning and cook for a few more minutes over medium heat. Pour in enough water or stock to make a soft mixture and chill until needed. When ready to use place a spoonful of mixture in the middle of each pastry circle and brush with a little egg yolk along the edges. Press together firmly and deep fry until golden.

To make the pastry: Dust flour on table together with salt and egg and mix well. Pour in oil and water and knead into a dough. Rest at room temperature for 30 minutes.

Roll out thinly and cut into circles, then fill with stuffing.

MAKES 10

Recipe © Macau Government Tourist Office, used with permission..

PRAWN AND RICE VERMICELLI SOUP (SOPA LACASSÁ)

200g (7oz) rice vermicelli
2 tablespoons olive oil
1 cup chopped onions
2 green onions, chopped
2 bay leaves
1 red chilli
1 lemon, sliced
2 tablespoons Chinese wine
30g (1oz) shrimp paste
12 cups (3pts) fish stock
300g (10½oz) peeled green prawns (shrimps)
salt and pepper to taste

   Soak vermicelli in cold water until soft. Heat olive oil in a large pot and add onions (leaving some aside for garnish), bay leaves, chilli and lemon. Add Chinese wine and shrimp paste and stir fry for five minutes until fragrant. Add fish stock and prawns and cook for 10 minutes. Strain vermicelli and place it in the soup serving dish, pour the soup over it, then garnish with a sprinkle of chopped green onions.

SERVES 10

Recipe © Macau Government Tourist Office, used with permission..

the western region

SZECHUAN FOOD: HOT AND SPICY

FIERY FOOD FROM THE WEST

THIS IS THE REGION KNOWN BEST FOR ITS HOT FOOD AND INCLUDES THE PROVINCES OF HUNAN, YUNNAN AND SZECHUAN (SOMETIMES SPELLED SICHUAN), WITH CHENGDU ITS CAPITAL.

The mighty Yangtse river wanders through this central area of China but nothing really explains why dishes here vibrate with the zing of chillies and those lip-numbing Szechuan peppers as well as cassia bark, cumin, cinnamon, peppercorns, star anise, and dried tangerine peel.

Nor is it known how chillies—which now grow prolifically all over the region— arrived at this remote mountain-ringed province in the first place, although it had to be some time after

their discovery in the New World by Christopher Columbus. Some say that Buddhist missionaries from India or Spanish traders carried them into China along the Silk Road to the north. Others favour the theory that they were introduced to Chinese merchants trading with Portuguese and Spanish sailors.

The climate in this region, far inland, is often hot and humid. Maybe it was this that created a liking for spicy foods which many other tropical equatorial countries also favour.

Mao Zedong preferred the food of his home region, Hunan, which has some subtle differences to dishes from the other regions, including the use of fresh chillies instead of dried ones. The fertile Middle Yangtze Plain lies in northeastern Hunan and is famous for its agriculture. Hunan cuisine is also known for the increased preparation times needed for dishes, often due to the lengthy marination of meats or double cooking of some dishes. Even with its reputation for incendiary combinations, it is interesting that not all Szechuan dishes are spicy. In fact the most highly spiced dishes are routinely reserved for home meals, with banquet dishes being more moderately spiced.

Perhaps more noticeable in this cuisine is the inclusion of a range of many flavours—sweet, sour, bitter, hot, salty, aromatic, and fragrant. No doubt this plays off the factor that a prime effect of chilli is that it acts to stimulate the palate, making it more sensitive to other flavours. If you have ever paired chilli with chocolate, for example, you will know the truth of this.

Chilli is meant to work as a palate cleanser, too, although anyone who has had their tastebuds all but blown away by too much of it might vigorously dispute this—once their power of speech returns!

SICHUAN CHICKEN AND HOT PEPPERS (SICHUAN JIDANG)

400g (14oz) chicken breast
1 teaspoon dark soy sauce
2 teaspoons rice wine
1 teaspoon fine white sugar
2 garlic cloves, crushed
1 tablespoon vegetable oil
2–3 teaspoons sesame oil
½ red capsicum (bell pepper), finely shredded
2 green onions, shredded
1 large green chilli, seeded and finely shredded
1 hot red chilli, seeded and finely shredded
1 teaspoon Sichuan peppercorns, crushed
1 tablespoon light soy sauce or oyster sauce
⅔ cup (160ml/5½ fl oz) chicken stock or water
1½ teaspoons cornflour

Thinly slice the chicken and cut into strips.

Place in a bowl to marinate for 15 minutes with the dark soy sauce, rice wine, sugar and garlic.

Heat the vegetable and sesame oils in a wok, and when smoking stir-fry the capsicum, onion and chillies for 40 seconds.

Push vegetables to the side of the pan and stir-fry the chicken until pale and firm, about 1 minute.

Season with the peppercorns and soy sauce, stirring well.

Combine chicken stock with cornflour and stir in to thicken.

SERVES 4

Recipe © Jacki Passmore, used with permission.

BAMBOO AND BICYCLES

THE CHINESE NAME FOR PANDA TRANSLATES AS 'GIANT CAT BEAR' AND WE COULD SEE WHY WHEN WE ROUNDED A CORNER AT THE BEIJING ZOO AND ENCOUNTERED SEVERAL LAZY GREAT BLACK AND WHITE CREATURES STRETCHING VOLUPTUOUSLY ON THEIR LOG PERCHES. IT WAS OBVIOUS THEY HAD NO IDEA HOW IMPORTANT THEY WERE, OR THEIR TASK IN KEEPING AN ENDANGERED SPECIES ALIVE.

Today only something like 3000 pandas live in the wild with another couple of hundred around the world in captivity. But there they were, oblivious to all the fuss, gnawing on bunches of tender bamboo leaves and soaking up the sunshine and the tourist attention.

It must be quite a task keeping the food up to these animals as an adult panda will consume up to 12 to 15 kilograms (26-33lbs) of bamboo branches, stems and leaves daily, although it is said they can eat up to a whopping 38 kilograms (83lbs), or around 40 per cent of their average body weight. Maybe it's something in bamboo that contributes to the pandas' benign personalities, for they are nothing like their cousins, grizzlies and polar bears. Instead they appear more like the toy members of the clan—teddy bears.

Male pandas of this species are truly 'giant', weighing up to 115 kilograms (253lbs) with the females a little lighter. Giant Pandas live in the mountainous regions of

China: Sichuan, Gansu, Shaanxi, and Tibet. Chengdu, in Szechuan province, is the epicentre of panda life, and the location of the world-famous Research Base of Giant Panda Breeding.

My memories of Chengdu have nothing to do with pandas though. We had arrived after a spectacular flight from Lhasa over mountains and more mountains, then descended into a bowl of white goo which was Chengdu. The air was so thick you could cut it, and this city has a population of 12 million people. One of them, our guide, denied the pollution was normal, but others we asked wagged their heads sadly and told us otherwise.

Outside our hotel a space on the roadside was packed solid with parked bicycles. This city could be called Cycle Central as there must be thousands, possibly millions of bikes, in Chengdu. We'd found the trip from the airport a totally hair raising experience and I couldn't imagine what it might be like to live here and attempt to commute in such crazy traffic. Suddenly, it seemed those fluffy black and white beauties chilling out with a stalk of bamboo had to be the most sensible of us all.

FISH FRAGRANT EGGPLANT

In Sichuan, there are a range of dishes which emulate the fragrance of fish because the condiments used to flavour them are traditionally used for cooking fish. Blending garlic, ginger, spring onions and Sichuan chilli bean paste, these dishes are truly a joy to eat. In this dish, the eggplants are deep-fried to a buttery tenderness and are simply delectable.

2 eggplants (aubergines)
Vegetable or olive oil for deep-frying
1½ tablespoons Sichuan chilli paste—to taste
3 teaspoons garlic, finely chopped
3 teaspoons ginger, finely chopped
2/3 cup (5fl oz/160ml) chicken stock
1 tablespoon shaoxing wine
1½ teaspoons sugar
1 teaspoon light soy sauce
1 teaspoon corn flour mixed with 1 tablespoon water
1½ teaspoons Chinkiang vinegar
3 spring onions (shallots, scallions), green parts only, finely sliced

Cut the eggplants in half lengthways and then crosswise. Slice each quarter into 4–5 evenly-sliced chunks. Slice again into 7–8cm pieces.

In your wok, heat oil for deep-frying. Deep-fry eggplant, in batches, until golden and soft. Remove and drain on kitchen paper. (this step can be done a few hours ahead if preferred)

Drain off deep-frying oil. Rinse or wipe-dry with kitchen paper. Heat again and add 2–3 tablespoons oil. Add the chill paste and fry for about 20 seconds, then add garlic and ginger. Take care to avoid burning—move wok from heat if need be. Add the stock, sugar, soy sauce, then the eggplant. Simmer a few minutes to allow flavours to blend. Check seasoning. Gently stir in corn flour to thicken the sauce, and then add the vinegar and spring onion, reserving 1 tablespoon for garnish. Serve and scatter spring onion over the top.

Note: Sichuan chilli paste (sichuan la jiao jiang) is made with ground chillies, salt and yellow bean or broad bean paste. The most popular is the famous Pixian chilli bean paste. It is sold in Minh Phat or any Chinese grocer.

SERVES 6 AS PART OF A MULTI-COURSE MEAL

Recipe © Tony Tan, used with permission, www.tonytan.com.au

TENDER SHOOTS

PANDAS ARE NOT THE ONLY ANIMALS THAT LIKE BAMBOO. AT LEAST IN CHINA, HUMANS ARE PRETTY FOND OF THE TENDER SHOOTS AS WELL.

Bamboo tips, low in kilojoules, high in potassium, are available fresh or canned. If bought fresh, they must be cooked as they are unappealingly bitter (and possibly toxic) when raw. Crisp and tender like asparagus when cooked, with a flavour similar to corn, they are delicious sliced and added to stir-fried dishes.

While I knew about these, I was unprepared at breakfast on Yellow Mountain south of Shanghai to find my 'zongzi', a steamed dumpling of glutinous rice filled with some tasty savoury mixture, wrapped in bamboo leaves. It came tightly bound by threads and I learned these little packages enclose a typical dish in southern and eastern China.

Bamboo is one of the Four Noble Ones in Chinese culture (together with plum blossom, orchid and chrysanthemum) while with the pine tree and plum blossom, bamboo is included as one of the Three Friends in Winter because it can withstand harsh conditions. The Chinese see it as a symbol of longevity, no doubt because of its long life (around 75 years) but its rare flowering, only about twice a century, is an important omen. It is said to forecast famine.

Bamboo, a true grass, is indigenous to China, which is lucky for the pandas who eat little else. The resourceful Chinese however have found many other uses for it. Primitive fishermen might make rafts from lengths lashed together and in some parts strong poles make ideal scaffolding while the slimmer ones can be used for

fishing rods. It is valuable for treating infections and of course its strength and flexibility makes it ideal for houses, flooring, furniture, matches, toothpicks, T-shirts, hats, mats and shoes. Burn bamboo and its ash can be used as a deodoriser.

And what else is as good for making chopsticks?

CHILLI TOMATO EGGS (XI HONG SHI JAO JI DAN)

We ate this dish from one side of China to the other. It was delicious and very quick to prepare. While this recipe always appeared as part of a large selection of other dishes at Chinese meals, it would just as easily make a good breakfast dish or light meal.

1–2 tablespoons peanut or other cooking oil
1 onion, chopped
1–2 cloves garlic, crushed
1–2 small red chillies, according to taste, finely chopped
4 tomatoes, chopped
salt and freshly ground pepper to taste
6 eggs, well beaten

   Place the oil in a large heavy frying pan and heat. Add onion and garlic and cook, stirring, until onions are translucent. Add chilli and stir well, then reduce heat immediately and add tomatoes, cooking slowly until well cooked. Season to taste. Pour eggs into the tomato mixture and cover the pan, stirring just a couple of times more to break the eggs up a little, cooking until set like scrambled eggs. Serve immediately.

SERVES 4.

CHOPSTICKS

While Chinese dining is generally a relaxed, noisy, fun way to eat, there are some rules involved with the use of chopsticks.

This is the polite way to eat:

· Never pass food to someone else's chopsticks with your chopsticks or leave your chopsticks sticking up from food, especially rice. Both these actions are associated with death and funerals.

· When not eating, place your chopsticks in front of you with the tip facing left. They may be rested horizontally on the plate or bowl or on a chopstick rest.

· Use chopsticks like tongs to pick up pieces of food. Do not spear food with them. In certain cases they may be used to tear larger pieces of food to make it easier to eat.

· It is considered bad manners to wave chopsticks around, or use them to move plates, toy with food or point at others.

· If a serving plate has no serving spoon, use the thick end of your own chopsticks (rather than using the end you have been eating with) to serve yourself with food.

· It is good manners to lift a rice bowl in your left hand to your mouth and shovel the rice in with your chopsticks. Some Chinese do not like to see rice picked up in chopsticks.

· Keep your hand facing downwards when using chopsticks. Showing your palm is considered unrefined.

DID YOU KNOW?

A COMMON WEDDING PRESENT IN CHINA IS A SET OF CHOPSTICKS. NOT ONLY IS THIS PRACTICAL, BUT THE CHINESE WORD FOR CHOPSTICKS SOUNDS THE SAME AS 'SOON SON'.

Chopsticks originated in China almost 4,000 years ago and gained favour because they were regarded as more refined than using a knife. The reason for this was that scholars, who used pens, were deemed to deserve more respect than warriors whose power came from knives.

Around 45 billion pairs of disposable chopsticks are used and thrown away in China annually. This translates as 25 million fully grown trees each year, or many bamboo groves.

It is believed that silver chopsticks, easily blackened by dangerous metal oxides, were once used in the Chinese imperial palace to detect poisons in the Emperor's meals.

In some Asian electronics factories a simple test for employment, to check a potential worker's hand-eye coordination, is to ask them to pick up a small bead with chopsticks.

SPICY CHICKEN WITH PEANUTS (GONGBAO OR KING PAO CHICKEN)

A classic Western dish that probably originated in the north and is found in many other regions too. Substitute corn kernels, diced capsicum or carrot for the zucchini, depending on local availability.

2 tablespoons peanut oil
3 dried red chillies, split lengthways in half,
and seeds removed if preferred
500g (1lb) chicken breast, skin removed (or tenderloins)
cut into 1cm (½ in) cubes
1 cup roasted peanuts
1 small zucchini (courgette) cut into 1cm cubes
2 tablespoons chicken stock or water
2 tablespoons rice wine or dry sherry
1 tablespoon dark soy sauce
2 teaspoons sugar
1 tablespoon chopped garlic
¼ onion, finely chopped
1 teaspoon Chinese white rice vinegar or white vinegar
1 teaspoon salt
2 teaspoons sesame oil, to serve

Heat a wok over high heat. Add oil and chillies and stir fry briefly, removing chillies when they are dark. Add chicken, peanuts and zucchini and stir for a minute, then remove and keep warm. Place all remaining ingredients except sesame oil in the wok. Bring to the boil, stirring, then return the chicken mixture to the wok and cook for three or four minutes. Drizzle with sesame oil and serve immediately.

SERVES 4.

PEPPERCORNS

A long way from anywhere on one trip, in Tianshui in Gansu province, almost dead centre of China, I thought I was having a stroke. My tongue felt thick and tingly and my lips suddenly became numb. I was even more concerned that Gordon was not showing the same symptoms. It must be me. I must have developed something dreadful, for sure, I thought.

But just before I lapsed into full-blown hypochondria, I replayed what I had just been doing. We were dining at a claypot restaurant and had been served a delicious dish of prawns (shrimps) and calamari (squid) with quail eggs. The sauce was silky and fragrant, studded with small pinkish dried berry-like things which seemed to have been deep-fried and were addictively crunchy. I liked them so much I had been picking them out and nibbling on them when I suddenly developed these strange symptoms.

Having discovered the cause, I still did not know if this was an allergic reaction or not. Of course time proved it wasn't as my mouth returned to normal by the end of the meal but I had to wait until I was home in Australia again before I could research

my mystery assailant properly. I discovered I had been hit by Szechuan peppercorns, or 'Zanthoxylum piperitum', not true peppercorns, but rather the shells from the berry of the prickly ash tree, often ground and used as a component of five-spice powder.

Of course I also quickly learned that the reaction I had experienced was quite common. In fact the Chinese believe 'ma la' (the term used to describe the numb-hot effect of these 'peppercorns') is good for the health in cold and wet weather. Certainly, until Columbus brought back chillies from the new world, they provided one of the few ways to spice up food.

Most cooks lightly toast and then crush the pods discarding the inedible seeds before adding them to food, usually at the last moment. Because they flourish in colder climates and at high altitudes, these berries also appear in Tibetan recipes, often used to flavour the local stuffed dumplings called 'momos'. Tibetans believe that Szechuan peppers can protect diners if unfresh meat is used, but others say it simply masks any 'off' flavours, which can make it useful for offal dishes.

the far western region

TIBET AND THE SILK ROAD:
SIMPLE HEARTY FOOD

THE FOOD OF
THE FAR WEST

ALTHOUGH NOT ONE OF THE FOUR
MAIN CUISINES OF CHINA, THE FOOD
OF THE FAR WEST IS SUFFICIENTLY
INTERESTING TO MENTION DUE
TO THE RESULT OF SEVERAL
INFLUENCES.

To the north and north-west the preferences
of the local Muslim population, the Uyghurs,
is responsible for the use of mutton, lamb and
beef on menus and the almost total absence of
pork products. Indeed there are many Muslim
restaurants which offer entirely halal dining.

In these regions the food may be less showy
and complex than on the coast, but it is hearty
and tasty, and large wheels of crusty bread called
'nang' can be bought anywhere.

Even so, some things are not to everyone's taste.
Without warning on a walk through the Kashgar
market, for instance, you might come upon a vat
heaped with boiled sheep's heads or the offer of a
take-away dish of plain noodles enhanced by thick
slabs of fat, chilli and pickled vegetables.

Ramadan is also observed in these areas and
during this period the usual daytime meals and
snacks may not be available, although locals can
be seen hauling off freshly killed carcasses from
the markets. These no doubt will be roasted and
devoured by devotees as soon as they may officially
break their fasts, when the day closes.

Despite the desert conditions grapes and other
fruits are grown in this area once thronged by

merchants on the Silk Road. Sultanas are dried in ventilated brick barns safely away from birds and other vermin. These as well as nuts and other dried fruit are for sale in every market and make the ideal snack food for travellers.

To the south-west on the high Tibetan plateau, the altitude and bitter conditions, as well as the predominantly Buddhist religion define the cuisine. The local form of Buddhism forbids the eating of small animals such as fish and poultry, but allows the slaughter and use of large animals, so yak, tasting remarkably like beef, appears in many curries and stews.

Roasted barley flour from the local highland grain appears in tsampa, a sort of dough and is also used to brew alcohol. Cabbages and other cool-climate vegetables grow well in the warmer months and yak milk is used for making yoghurts and cheeses.

Then there is butter tea, a curiously popular smoky brew made by churning yak butter with tea in a tall pot, the resultant flavour depending entirely on the freshness of the butter.

TIBET ON THE HORIZON

TIBET CAME TO MEET US, IT SEEMED.
MANY KILOMETRES ON THE CHINESE
SIDE OF THE BORDER THE LANDSCAPE,
PEOPLE AND BUILDINGS CHANGED
SUDDENLY.

Now we drove past villages of neat whitewashed adobe and drystone houses and hay racks standing like artists' easels in the fields, then soon found ourselves rising high above the squares of cultivated vegetables, barley, and grass, and the semi-permanent lakes and hillsides criss-crossed by tiny paths, both human and animal. Finally we learned to identify yaks: large black beasts with

formidable upward pointing horns and shaggy tails. It was rockier now too, the bare cliff tops like cutouts against a calendar-blue sky.

This was isolated country yet there were plenty of animals on the roadside—black pigs, hens, pack-saddled donkeys—and local people. The men wore a black fedora-style hat with a flat brim, a confusing similarity between Tibetans and South Americans, and there were monks too, in

maroon and cerise robes.

At one village a group of people sat around a well with spring water spouting all over the pigs that were happily sploshing around. At another, higher still, a group of men played snooker outside a cafe, oblivious to the stunning backdrop of snowy mountains. Beyond this, still climbing, we passed our first nomad camp of black tents. We had definitely arrived in Tibet whatever the map said.

We ate lunch that day seated at low tables on a bare concrete floor in a dingy little restaurant—the sort you would never be game to enter on your own— yet our meal of greens and chilli, tomato and egg, and roast pork was fresh and tasty.

Then we were climbing steadily onwards between slopes covered with rhododendrons, snowcapped peaks beyond, pausing briefly at a pass where the lookout sign ordered in Chinese: 'Keep Quiet, No Hunting'. They didn't need to tell us. We were speechless.

A little later we saw Mei Ling Snow Mountain in the distance, a virgin (unclimbed) mountain. It is regarded as a holy mountain by Buddhists and at over 6774 metres (22,000 feet), the highest mountain in Yunnan. The Tibetans walk around it. believing they will be blessed.

At dusk we arrived at Deqen, at an altitude of 3000 metres (980 feet), close to the actual border between China and Tibet. It felt like a wild west town—a real frontier town. I almost expected to see a shootout in the saloon, but instead the foyer of our hotel had pictures of palms and sandy beaches and Niagara Falls.

Such is China.

STEAMED TIBETAN MOMOS OR CHINESE DUMPLINGS

Momos are very similar to Chinese wontons and other dumplings and you may decide if you want to cook the meat to be used in the filling before steaming the filled dumplings. They may also be pan-fried, instead of steaming, for about the same length of time, if preferred, taking care they do not stick, by adding a little more oil or water as necessary.

Mashed tofu or chopped and lightly sautéed vegetables such as cabbage, carrots, broccoli and herbs may be substituted for meat when serving vegetarians. A mix of well-spiced cooked potato filling makes an excellent Samosa-like momo. While you may make your own wrappers using the recipe below, commercially available gow gee wrappers make the task a little easier.

WRAPPERS

1 cup flour
pinch of salt
water
vegetable, canola or sunflower cooking oil

FILLING

½ cup finely chopped onion
2 cloves of garlic, chopped finely
250g (8oz) pork or other meat mince
1 tablespoon soy sauce
chilli sauce to taste
salt and freshly ground pepper to taste

Mix flour and salt, adding a little water at a time to make a stiff dough. Leave to stand while making filling.

Heat oil in a pan and fry onion until translucent. Add garlic and fry until just turning golden. Add the meat and cook until browning, then add soy and chilli sauces, mixing well. Season to taste and finish cooking the meat.

Divide the dough into equal-sized balls and roll into thin circles approximately 10cm (8in) in diameter, stretching the edges slightly to make them thinner than the centre.

Brush edges with water and place a tablespoon-full of filling in the centre. Fold each circle in half to make a semi-circle and pinch the edges firmly, pleating for an attractive effect. Small inexpensive plastic presses are available in Asian markets that will do this more easily. Place gently in a well-oiled steamer making sure the dumplings do not touch, then steam for 10–15 minutes. Serve hot with chutney and a clear soup such as Thukpa for a Tibetan-style meal, or with any other broth or soup and dipping sauces.

SERVES 4.

FACES OF TIBET

THE COLOURFUL KHAMPA PEOPLE LIVE ON THE EASTERN THIRD OF THE TIBETAN PLATEAU COVERING PARTS OF THE TAR (TIBET AUTONOMOUS REGION), SICHUAN, QINGHAI AND YUNNAN.

These people are swashbuckling cowboys, daring horsemen and wear either a traditional cowboy hat or skeins of red or black threads looped into a sort of turban. They look fierce, especially with those large knives hanging from their belts, but we found them to be more fascinated by our strange white faces, and keen to communicate whatever way they could.

Shortly after crossing the Tibetan border north of Deqen, we continued northwards until we reached Markham, a rather untidy town with a drain running down the centre of the muddy main street. We stopped at the far end of town and attempted to talk to the local people who all seemed to be Khampas. We then made the connection. Of course! This town didn't have an English name at all, despite the spelling and pronunciation. It was Mar-Kham.

These locals, while very friendly, didn't want their pictures taken. We pleaded with one young man wearing a wonderful moustache with waxed ends and he finally acquiesced. Around another corner a wizened old women sat in the sun spinning a prayer wheel and fingering a rosary, and we snapped her without her seeing us.

This area was quite high and the altitude was really getting to a few of us. So much so that whenever we walked anywhere we looked more like a bunch of convalescents hobbling slowly along in our attempts to conserve oxygen.

As we travelled on we passed huddles of whitewashed houses with bright painted designs under the eaves, around the windows and on the lintels and gates. We came upon a mother and son standing on the side of the road above a sickening drop to a thread of river hundreds of metres below. The little bloke was holding a turnip, so we took pictures and I gave him some gloves I had brought along, but then like kids anywhere, all that attention was too much for him and he started bawling.

These roads were truly terrifying. We seemed to be headed direct for the sky. You could look ahead and high up the hillsides see the stripes of what we knew was our road cut into them, equidistant above each other, switching backwards and forwards up what appeared to be an almost vertical mountain face. The road itself was notched with landslides and holes partially filled with rocks and the rubble that had come from above.

That evening at our campsite, I washed my hair in the mountain stream and I swear it was the coldest thing I have ever done.

As mother nature dried it for me I wrote in my diary: 'What sort of life is this? Sitting on a rock, with my feet amongst yak turds, beside a white water stream watching those black beasts plod slowly home to the nomads' tents on the opposite hill.'

TIBETAN BUTTER TEA

In Tibet, yak butter is pumped up and down with tea in deep cylindrical pots. It is impossible to replicate the smoky flavour that permeates it, nor would you want to introduce the rancidity of butter kept without refrigeration. The closest palatable version is this. Russian Caravan blend has a similar campfire quality to give you some idea of what this favourite Tibetan drink is like.

BUTTER TEA

Tibetans like their tea salty—that's right, salty—but make this to suit your own taste. It always has a smoky overtone due to the turf cooking fires in the nomad settlements.

4 cups (1 litre/32 fl oz) water
1 tablespoon Russian Caravan tea leaves
2 tablespoons cream
2 tablespoons milk
1 tablespoon butter
salt

Boil the water and tea together in a saucepan for about 10 minutes. Strain off the tea leaves and add cream, milk and butter, then salt to taste. Reheat the tea if desired, but do not boil. If you like frothy tea, pour it backwards and forwards between two jugs.

MAKES 4 CUPS

A REST BY A RIVER

ONE NIGHT IN TIBET WE STAYED IN A SIMPLE HOSTEL, THE SORT USED BY PILGRIMS MAKING THE LONG AND DEMANDING TREK TO LHASA. WE WOKE TO FIND YAKS GRAZING IN THE YARD AND A DOZEN DOGS DOZING IN THE SUNSHINE.

After a breakfast of fried egg with a hot fresh round Tibetan bread we made our way out of the tacky, dusty, smoky village of Bachan. The road here was very rough—we hadn't seen a sealed road in many days—although around us the terrain had smoothed out and we were in bare land, rather moor-like and covered with golden green grass.

A few kilometres from the town our convoy of 4WDs was stopped by a landslide, a small one, but it took the drivers a few minutes to clear. Our vehicle was last and when we reached the next town where we had hoped to see a sandalwood monastery, we found the lead cars had been accosted by the military police and almost forced to go to the police station.

Fortunately they resisted and by the time we turned up, the officers had calmed down and only wanted to check our passports, although we were still made to wait about an hour before they told us we could not see the monastery in any case. All the time this was going on we were surrounded by brightly dressed Khampa and other locals, staring and sticking their heads in the car windows. Such curiosities, these foreign visitors. I'm sure they wished they had cameras too, so they could take pictures of us!

We pushed on, making camp early beside a startlingly

turquoise river. As usual it was only moments before a friendly
nomad family came to check us out—Grandma, a young mum
and the kids. We always found these people so quiet and fearless.
They would simply infiltrate our group and stand beside us, quietly
absorbing it all. The mother settled down to feed the youngest
on the bank in front of us without any shyness, while the others
offered us to sell us turquoise and what appeared to be ivory, but
was more likely yak bone.

Around us marmots were everywhere, dashing down their
little burrows as soon as we approached. Little sandpiper-like birds
often confused us into thinking they were marmots too as they
hopped amongst the tall grass.

Meanwhile an old lady with cropped white hair and a deeply
lined yet serene face silently came up and sat on the hillside
overlooking the tents, spinning her prayer wheel in the fading light.

FORBIDDEN CITY

WE ARRIVED AT LHASA IN TIME TO
VISIT THE JOKHANG, THE MAIN TEMPLE
IN THE CITY, THE MOST REVERED
RELIGIOUS STRUCTURE IN TIBET.
WE DISCOVERED IT WAS A DOUBLY
AUSPICIOUS DAY—THE 30TH DAY OF
THE EIGHTH MONTH.

Everywhere people were lighting butter lamps
with ghee they had bought outside the temple.
Their excitement was evident as they pressed hard
together, clinging to each other's shoulders, the
eagerness at finally entering this holy place evident
on their faces. Some would have travelled many
kilometres—and I realised we may have passed some
of them crammed onto the back of open 'buses', or
even a few coming the hardest way, by prostrating
themselves over and over: a million stony body
lengths to Lhasa.

The walls of our room in the aptly-named Yak
Hotel were decorated with amazing Tibetan naïve
art, the ceiling covered with a rich tile-like design and
baroque curlicues and swirling creatures. It seems

we hardly had time to appreciate it properly as there was so much else to see in Lhasa. Tibet's capital at an elevation of 3700 metres (12,000 feet), is one of the world's highest cities with, despite this, an average 3600 annual hours of sunshine.

Of course, on our first day we visited the 13-storey maroon and white Potala Palace with its 1000 rooms, rising supreme above the city, dominating and aloof, and perhaps even more stunning when seen from a distance. We spent a couple of hours there captivated by the interiors, clambering up stairs, enjoying the space and relative calm, as well as the views across the city. Its prominent position means that wherever you are in Lhasa there is usually a corner visible, and it stands as a solid reminder that Buddhism survives, despite the red and yellow flag flying over it.

Next to the Johkang, swept along by the tide of pilgrims, past the tall stone furnaces burning incense and juniper branches which give off the scent that is the signature of temples throughout China. I called it holy smoke.

Inside were many hundreds of people, a sort of religious gridlock, the crowd humming omani padani om, a booming tone which swelled to fill the space like a great organ. The air was cloudy with smoke and butter fat from the lamps, and I remember prayer mats, women with turquoise chunks anchored in their black hair lighting butter lamps with great concentration, and the sound of brass bells ringing.

Borne along by the crowds up stairs made slippery by splashes of yak butter, we finally made it to the rooftop and looked down on the forecourt of makeshift stalls selling drinks and biscuits and the mass of people prostrating themselves.

From there we could also see across to the Potala Palace, which we sighted again later from the roof of the Yak Hotel. Only then it was fittingly framed by prayer flags.

TOFFEE POTATOES

I couldn't believe my eyes when I first saw this dish. It is so unusual, yet quite delicious.

1kg (2lb) potatoes
3-4 tablespoons cooking oil, butter or ghee
salt to taste
1 cup sugar
½ cup water

Peel potatoes and cut into quarters. Boil until tender then drain thoroughly.

Heat oil, butter or ghee in a large heavy frypan and, when hot, add the potatoes, stirring until they are browning well. Season to taste with salt.

Meanwhile make toffee by placing the sugar and water in a small heavy pan. Cook, stirring occasionally until it becomes golden.

Place potatoes on individual plates or a serving dish and immediately pour some of the toffee lightly over the potatoes, enough so it is attractive but not so much as to form a hard shell.

SERVES 4

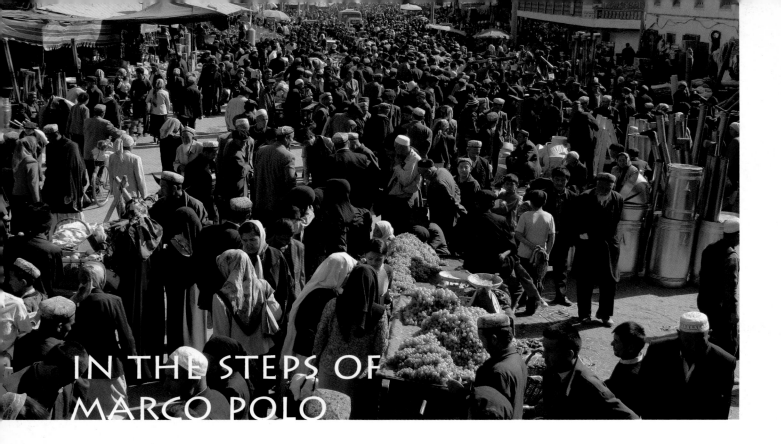

IN THE STEPS OF MARCO POLO

A TRIP ALONG CHINA'S ANCIENT SILK ROAD IS ONE OF THOSE ONCE-IN A LIFETIME DREAMS. THIS ROAD BEGAN WITH VISIONARIES AND THE EFFORTS OF THOSE WHO DARE.

Around the 23rd-century BC, Lei Zu, wife of the Yellow Emperor, Huang Di who ruled in mythical times, was seated under a mulberry tree in the palace gardens. With nothing better to do than fiddle with a silkworm cocoon above her, she began winding the fine, strong thread around her fingers and—the story goes—wondered if it might be woven into cloth.

Fast forward two thousand years, during which time the manufacture of silk had been perfected, to the second century BC. The current Emperor began to see an export chance and a hapless scout named Zhang was elected to be sent to see if a route to markets in the West could be found. He was captured, and it took him a mere twenty years to finally make it back with good news.

Like thousands before us we made the trip too, beginning far west in Kashgar, a town more Central Asian than Chinese, where we wandered unnoticed, despite being the only westerners, amongst camel, horse and donkey traders at the weekly Sunday markets. It was a sweaty, busy place, full of noise and action and we retreated later to the town's general markets to cool down with freshly squeezed pomegranate juice, sticky green figs and cake hacked from a large slab then iced on the spot for us.

North from there we visited the aptly named Heavenly Lake near Urumqi, and watched local horsemen thrill tourists with their skills. Zhang told the emperor he'd found 'heavenly horses' on his travels, perhaps exaggerating their prowess. It was a good

selling point though as horses were needed, along with camels and donkeys to carry the valuable burdens of the early caravans.

The Silk Road was really three roads, north, south and central, each torturous and dangerous, crossing deserts and mountains and some of the driest, deadliest country in the world. For a little added effect, factor in brigands poised to ambush the weary merchants as they travelled. The ultimate destination was the Mediterranean where this mystery fabric was a hot favourite for everything from regal robes to royal underwear.

Nor was it a one-way street. While China had paper, furs, jade, tea, gunpowder, and compasses, the west responded with fast horses, gold, ivory, precious metals, tapestries, and much more. Buddhism hitched a ride east with the caravans too.

The early Silk Road was a noisy, bustling thoroughfare filled with movement and a constantly passing crowd of people along that vast artery crossing most of the then-known world. It is not much different now. Today's camels are battered faded-blue trucks their loads covered with black tarpaulins.

THUKPA

This soup may be made spicier by adding crushed chilli, and other vegetables such as potato, tomato and spinach can also be added. If using potatoes, cook them first or allow the soup to cook for longer.

2 tablespoons butter, ghee or cooking oil
2 cloves garlic, crushed
½ onion, finely chopped
4 cups (1-1¾pt) chicken, beef or vegetable stock
salt or soya sauce and freshly ground pepper to taste
1 tablespoon grated ginger
2 eggs lightly beaten
1-2 cups fresh egg noodles, cooked
finely chopped coriander leaves, to garnish

Heat butter, ghee or oil in a large saucepan and fry garlic briefly, then add onion and cook until tender.

Add stock, season to taste and add ginger, then simmer for ten minutes.

Pour eggs into the soup and whisk well to break them into strands as they cook.

Place some noodles in each bowl and pour the soup over them. Add coriander and serve immediately with dumplings.

SERVES 4

A few notes about ingredients and cooking times

MEASUREMENTS ARE BASED ON AUSTRALIAN STANDARD MEASURES:

1 teaspoon is 5ml

1 tablespoon is 20ml (1 UK/US tablespoon is 15 ml/3 teaspoons)

1 cup is 250ml

The conversions given in the recipes in this book are approximate. If you have a set of scales then use the weight shown for the ingredients rather than the 'cups' equivalent. Please bear in mind that cooking times can vary depending on your appliance. The Celsius and Fehrenheit temperature in this book apply to most electric ovens.

Some standard conversions are

WEIGHTS			VOLUME		
Imperial	Metric		1fl oz	30ml	
1/2oz	15g		4fl oz	125ml	1/2 cup
1oz	30g		8fl oz	250ml	1 cup
5oz	150g		16fl oz	500ml	2 cups
10oz	300g		32fl oz	1 litre	4 cups
16oz(1lb)	500g				
2lb	1kg				

First published in Australia in 2007 by
New Holland Publishers (Australia) Pty Ltd
Sydney · Auckland · London · Cape Town

1/66 Gibbes Street Chatswood NSW 2067 Australia
218 Lake Road Northcote Auckland New Zealand
86 Edgware Road London W2 2EA United Kingdom
80 McKenzie Street Cape Town 8001 South Africa

National Library of Australia Cataloguing-in-Publication Data:
Hammond, Sally,
    Bamboo : a journey in Chinese food
    ISBN 9781741105698 (pbk.).
    1. Cookery, Chinese. 2. Cookery - China. 3. Tourism and
    gastronomy - China. 4. China - Description and travel. I.
    Title.
    641.5951

Publisher: Martin Ford
Project Editor: Lliane Clarke
Designer: Barbara Cowan
Food Photography: Vicki Liley, www.vickililey.com.au
Photography: Gordon Hammond, www.gordonhammond.com.au
Production Manager: Linda Bottari
Printer: C&C Offset Printing Co Ltd (China)

10 9 8 7 6 5 4 3 2 1

ACKNOWLEDGEMENTS

Many thanks to Helen Wong of Helen Wong's Tours (www.helenwongstours.com. au). Without you and your team's efficiency and help we would have seen so little of China, and understood less. Also to Tashi Lachman from Thor World Travel (www. thorworldtravel.com) our indefatigable guide into Tibet on our first-ever trip to China, thank you for gently introducing us to this wonderful place. Grateful thanks too for the generosity of several leading food writers: Pauline Loh, Gina Choong, Jacki Passmore, Carol Selva Rajah, Tony Tan and Ping Yan Yeung, and the Macau Government Tourist Office.